UNMASKING SECRETS
to
UNSTOPPABLE RELATIONSHIPS

How to Find, Keep, and Renew Love and Passion in Your Life

Lori Ann Davis, MA, CRS

Published by Lori Ann Davis, MA, CRS

Design and production by SPARK Publications
www.SPARKpublications.com

Visit lorianndavis.com to contact the author.

Printing History
Edition One, May 2015

ISBN: 978-0-692-38528-9

Unmasking Secrets to Unstoppable Relationships
How to Find, Keep, and Renew Love and Passion in Your Life

Dedication

I dedicate this book to you, the reader. May the
ideas in this book help you to create a relationship
that is better than you ever thought possible.

This book is written for:

This book is written for my three lovely daughters,
Michelle, Melissa, and Lauren. My wish for you is to
experience all the love and passion life has to offer. My
hope is that these secrets will help you on your journey
to creating your own unstoppable relationships.

With Gratitude:

To my extraordinary and loving Daddy, Granny, and Pa-Pa,
you showed me what true love really is. You were living examples
of what is possible in life and in love. I love you and miss you.

To Mike, our twenty-five years together are ones
I will never forget. Much of the information in this
book comes from our wonderful life together. Our
journey brought me to where I am today.

To Dave, you are my future. You have given me a second
chance at love. Your support and encouragement has meant
the world to me. I am very blessed to have you in my life.

Table of Contents

Secret #1: Unstoppable Desire

Make Your Relationship a Safe Haven
Pathway to Happiness
Random Acts of Kindness

Secret #2: Unstoppable Understanding

Men and Women: We Are Different
Get the Love You Want and Become Irresistible to Him
Make Him Feel Like Superman
Unleash Your Feminine Energy and Reclaim Passion

Secret #3: Unstoppable Communication

End Power Struggles
More Differences Between Men and Women

Secret #4: Unstoppable Love and Passion

It All Begins with You
Reignite Passion
Sexy Nights

Relationships take intention,
determination, the right attitude,
commitment, and effort,
but the results are worth it!

Preface

I met my ex-husband when I was twenty-two years old, and it was love at first sight. We had all of the aspects of an unstoppable relationship for twenty-five years! This took intention, determination, the right attitude, commitment, and effort, but the results were worth it every single day! Does that mean we had an easy life with no struggles? Of course not! We had our share of tragedies and difficulties over the years. There were times when I worked two jobs, and so did he. We had three children together over those years and our share of ups and downs.

Eventually, we found that we could not remain together, not because our relationship failed but because we had changed and grown into different people who were no longer right for each other. Not all relationships are meant to last forever, and sometimes the best path is to go your own separate ways. At first this was devastating for me because it meant losing my best friend of twenty-five years and my unstoppable relationship that I thought would last forever. I was not sure how to carry on without this wonderful man in my life. It was the hardest thing I have ever had to face. But I learned so much from that relationship, and that is what I will take away from it and share with you. It is because of this relationship that I have now dedicated my career to helping YOU find, keep, and renew love and passion in your life. It is my hope that this book will help you on your journey to a life that is better than you could have ever imagined.

My four secrets to an unstoppable relationship have come from my own experiences as well as what I have learned working with clients for over twenty-eight years. I will show you how to create an unstoppable relationship, how to understand the differences between men and women, how to end power struggles, and finally how to have unstoppable love and passion in your relationship. In my marriage, our relationship was a priority for both of us. We enjoyed a lot of activities together, more than most couples probably do, but we also kept our own interests and had the freedom to pursue new things separately. This really does keep the marriage alive and interesting. It took work, but we were able to keep the love and passion alive in our relationship all those years.

So after recovering from the loss of my marriage, I was ready to move forward, take everything I had learned, and apply it to my next relationship. I did not focus on the negatives but instead learned all I could so I could create an even better relationship the next time around. I now have a new guy in my life and am working on my next unstoppable relationship. I am no different than you; I have had great times as well as challenges in my life, but I realize that I am in control of creating the life I deserve, and I am here to help you do the same.

Through this book, I hope to show you how to create a relationship that is better than you could have ever imagined. No matter where you are in your current relationship, the secrets in this book will guide you even if you find that the best path is to move on and start over. This book will help you learn how to create an unstoppable relationship the next time around. It can help you heal and grow and be ready for the next phase of your life. I have learned so much from my first marriage as well as from my clients, and I am passionate about sharing that information with you. I learned that I have the power to create the kind of relationship I want, and that power also lies within YOU. Let's get started on your personal journey to an unstoppable relationship!

YOU have the power
to change your relationship. With
just a few secrets, you can create a
relationship you deserve, the one you
have always dreamed of.

Introduction

Relationships are something we are all a part of. They bring us comfort, happiness, and unity. We are part of work relationships, friendships, families, and, of course, romantic love relationships. Every relationship takes time and effort. They require give and take to keep them strong. Sometimes we are able to maintain a connection with others for years, and sometimes people move in and out of our lives rather quickly. And—let's face it—sometimes our relationships can cause us grief, stress, or frustration. So why do we work so hard to make someone else happy? Why do we endure the stress and compromise? Simply put, we long to feel connected to another human being. Those connections, though sometimes difficult, can ultimately affect how we feel about our work, our lives, and ourselves in general. We want to feel needed, loved, and cared for. As well, we long to provide that for someone else, which is why we seek intimate relationships. Creating and maintaining an intimate relationship can be one of the most rewarding experiences of our lives, but just like every other relationship, it requires effort and sometimes guidance.

When it comes to our intimate relationships, we all want a relationship that others notice and envy, a relationship that stands the test of time, one that is unstoppable. You know—that couple that seems to be so close, in love, and happy. You have no doubt that they are completely in love and committed to one another! We can all have that kind of relationship, but it doesn't just happen; it takes work, commitment, and know-how.

Bringing two people together from varying backgrounds with different personalities to form a family can bring its own set of challenges. No one teaches us how to have a relationship that is strong and healthy or how to have a relationship full of love and passion. Some are blessed with positive role models such as parents or family members that have strong foundations full of respect and love. This can offer insight into what they may want in future relationships. Others aren't as fortunate and may be exposed to unhealthy, unhappy relationships that ultimately end. Those people may think that a healthy, lasting relationship is impossible and that marriage is not supposed to last. They may believe that they cannot maintain that level of happiness over time with one partner, a mindset that is simply not true.

The ultimate goal of any intimate relationship is to get to a point where there is balance between friendship and passion, what I call the unstoppable stage. I believe that most people are satisfied with a good relationship because they do not believe anything more is possible. They really feel that they have it all and do not know any better, or they do not believe that anything more is a realistic expectation.

Sadly, those people enter a stale stage in their relationships. They may be communicating well and managing conflicts, but they are missing the passion that they desire. Or perhaps the intimacy is there, but they are not communicating effectively, and conflicts are creating a wedge. Or perhaps they feel stuck in their relationships, feeling like there is no hope. They may feel like their partners will never change, so there is nothing they can do.

One person can shift the relationship, and it can be either partner. You have the power to change your relationship for the better. This book will show you how. That said, I've written this book primarily for women who want to proactively enhance their relationships, with or without the buy-in of their partners. Ladies, I encourage you to share this book with your partners. Men reading this book can find value in it as well through gaining a better understanding of themselves and what is important to them. They will learn valuable information about how women think and what they want from men, as well as tools to better communicate with you.

This book will unmask secrets and provide you with tools that you can use immediately to start out on the right path or to find your way back to the place where it all started. I talk throughout the book about the characteristics of men and women. I am speaking in general terms that apply to most men and women. I do realize that not everyone fits into the mold.

Some men and women may be atypical. If you find this true about your situation, that is okay. Relationships work just as well if the roles are reversed in some areas, as long as both partners are in agreement. You can still use the information in this book to create an unstoppable relationship. Yours just might look a little different on the outside. The underlying principles of the book will still apply to you.

You will learn how to communicate effectively with your partner and why the way men and women think can be crucial to how you relate to one another day-to-day and in the bedroom! You will learn how to break the cycle of waiting for your partner to make changes in order for your relationship to improve. YOU have the power to change your relationship. Relationships can be complicated, but yours doesn't have to be. With just a few secrets, you can create a relationship you deserve, the one you have always dreamed of but weren't sure was possible, one that is unstoppable!

The first step is to learn to become the best partner you can be. This will take work on your part. You will have to examine your thoughts, beliefs, and actions. Which ones are not moving you forward on your path to the relationship you desire? This takes intention and soul searching. You will become not only the best partner you can be but also a happier person in the process. By becoming the best partner you can be, you will bring out the best in you and your partner.

Does this sound like the kind of relationship you would like to have? My hope is that by now you are interested enough and willing to consider that this is a possibility, even for you. I promise you that it is attainable, and this information will help you create the relationship you have always desired but were not sure was possible. This book is the combination of years of research, hours spent working with clients as a counselor for over twenty-eight years, and my own personal life journey.

Although we do not have the power
to always choose life's events,
we do have the power to choose
how we interpret them.

Is Your Past Haunting Your Current Relationship?

Everyone comes into relationships with a past. This past can bring with it unresolved issues that can affect the health of current relationships. This past might include your family of origin or previous intimate relationships. How does your life story affect your relationship story, and how similar are the two?

We all have losses in our lives when it comes to relationships. We all have a first love that we will never forget. Unless you are one of those few people who married your first love, this is probably the case for you. Even your current relationships can have painful moments. I do not think anyone is free from some kind of past hurt in regard to relationships. These past experiences (whether they are from your family of origin, past relationship losses, or events from your current relationship) can cause negative thoughts and beliefs that can affect your current happiness. It will also affect your happiness in the future if not dealt with.

Although we do not have the power to always choose life's events, we do have the power to change how we interpret them. There is a saying you may have heard: people come into our lives for a reason, a season, or a lifetime. Relationships are in our lives for different reasons; some are meant to be forever, and some only serve a purpose and run their course. Relationships are the main avenue for us to learn life lessons. Some people are just not meant to stay in our lives for as long as we would like. They teach us more by leaving than by staying. Failed relationships provide important lessons, and those lessons are gifts if we choose to receive them. If we can't let go, this is what causes pain. It is important to accept the lesson, love the person for what they provided, and learn for the future. Have you learned from your past and moved forward, or do you have some thoughts and beliefs that you are carrying with you that do not serve you well?

Past relationships are not the only places we learn lessons and collect beliefs regarding relationships. Our families of origin, or the people we grew up with, are where we learn so much about how to be in a relationship. For better or for worse, we learn beliefs and attitudes that affect our actions in current relationships. We learn what roles to play and what we expect from each other in a family. We learn how affection and anger are shown. We learn how to handle disagreements and money issues. We develop our beliefs and attitudes about marriage and family. As we get out in the world, we may alter these beliefs depending upon how we felt about our experiences growing up and what experiences we have in our adult relationships.

When you enter into a new relationship, both individuals bring their relationship histories, whether consciously or unconsciously. If you pick a partner who has similar beliefs and attitudes, usually the relationship is easier to navigate. Frequently, though, we don't even discuss these issues or find out what our beliefs are until they become a problem. Even then, you may not have awareness that your past is affecting the present. Understanding what you bring into the relationship can help you better understand your behavior and your partner's behavior. This awareness is key in helping you avoid negative patterns you have learned and leads to better choices and communication.

Whether it was a relationship that ended or a past issue from your current relationship, these events can lead to beliefs that ultimately inhibit your ability to create the unstoppable relationship you deserve. Let's take a minute and look at some of the beliefs you might be holding onto that could be hurting your current relationship:

- My parents aren't happily married, so I won't be either.
- I shouldn't have to work this hard. If we love each other, it should be easy.
- What happened in the past is what will happen in the future.

- I have to give up my friends or freedom when I get married.
- I see my friends unhappy, so I think everyone is unhappily married.
- I don't believe that a loving, passionate relationship is possible long-term.
- I can't be successful in business and happily married.
- Once children come along, they are the priority, and the marriage takes a back seat.
- I can't get the feelings back I once had.
- My partner won't change, so there is no hope for a future.
- No one is going to be faithful.
- All men cheat
- Men only care about sex.

These are just a few of the limiting beliefs many people have regarding relationships. These thoughts can be difficult to move past. I suggest you read these and make a list for yourself. Once you have identified your beliefs, write a list to replace them with more positive thoughts. For example, if you believe that you can't be successful in business and happily married, replace it with, "Having a happy marriage gives me energy and allows me to focus on being successful at work." Keep this list in your nightstand, in your purse, at your desk, in the bathroom, or any place you can look at it often and reread it! You want to replace the limiting beliefs with the ones that will help you have a better relationship. Here are a few more examples of positive beliefs that will help you. Use these as a guide to come up with your own list.

- With new tools and skills, I can have a different experience and create a better relationship.
- I can have a different relationship than my parents did.
- I am capable of change.
- I can change my relationship experience with or without my partner.
- It is possible to have a loving, passionate, long-term relationship.
- There are loving, caring, faithful partners, and I am one!

Letting go of past experiences and forgiving others and ourselves, including our parents, is an important part of moving forward. We are not taught how to accept a relationship or a person for what they have given us and then to move on. What did you learn from past relationships? What did you learn about yourself? What was the silver lining in these experiences? What role did you play? Take a look at your beliefs and attitudes that may be causing you difficulty; where did they come from? It is important to stop blaming others and take responsibility for your own actions. Even though you may be justified in your feelings of hurt, anger, or betrayal, carrying that with you will drag you down. It makes it hard, if not impossible, to move forward. Freedom comes from forgiving our past and ourselves. Marriage is only as healthy as the two people involved. Let go of past baggage and feel the huge weight lifted. Your marriage will be healthier and happier.

Exercise

Take some time now to do some soul searching in this area.
Make a list of hurts from past relationships or your current
relationship and answer these questions. See what patterns
emerge and what lessons you have learned or still need to learn.
Write more positive statements from what you have learned.
Don't allow past events and beliefs to keep you stuck. Don't let
negative thoughts and beliefs stay and determine your future.
YOU are in control of what you create in your life from now on!

- ❤ What did you learn from your past relationships?
- ❤ What did you learn about yourself?
- ❤ What was the silver lining in these experiences?
- ❤ What role did you play?
- ❤ What beliefs do you carry from these experiences?
- ❤ Make a list of positive beliefs to help you move forward.

Freedom comes from
forgiving our past and ourselves.
Let go of past baggage and feel
the huge weight lifted.

Small changes practiced
consistently will create big changes
in your life with your partner.

Relationships Don't Have to Be Scary!

So how do you get to that unstoppable place in your relationship? The first step is to consider what stage your relationship is in. Every relationship goes through several stages, which we will discuss in a moment. For now, let's start by assessing your relationship. Are you unhappy with the way things are going and wondering if the relationship can be saved? Are you relatively happy and thinking this is as good as it can get? Do you love your partner but miss the way things used to be when you had more love and passion in your relationship? Do you have a really good relationship but feel it could still be better? No matter where you are, this book can help you improve your relationship. Remember that it only takes one person to change a pattern.

My four secrets to creating unstoppable relationships start

on page 35. I hope you will read the whole book to get a feel for what areas you need to focus on. Keep this book on your bedside table and refer to it often. Start with one area and make small changes. Small changes practiced consistently will create big changes in your life with your partner. I will give you lots of tools you can implement right away to start improving your relationship. Try something small and see what happens. Then add something else and continue to work through the ideas in this book until you have that unstoppable relationship that you want and deserve.

Romantic Love

The first stage of a relationship is romantic love. Remember when you were first together and couldn't stop thinking about each other? You couldn't wait to see each other, you had to look your best, and your heart skipped a beat when he called. The beginning of a relationship is wonderful, exciting, and fun with all the chemistry flowing and those "feel good" hormones racing through your body. We sometimes call this the honeymoon phase. Generally, you see the best in the other person and look at them and the world through rose-colored glasses. It feels so good to know that this handsome guy is in love with you, and you love him in return! You want to spend all your time together, and usually your love life is full of passion! This phase will generally last from six months to two years before it starts to wear off. This is a natural progression and not something you have done wrong. The hormones that cause these wonderful feelings naturally start to decline. Frequently, people will make a permanent commitment or even get married during this phase. Remember the fairy tales that show the couple riding off into the sunset? Well, they are in this romantic phase, and that is all we are ever shown. The story doesn't continue, so we never learn what to expect next. We assume things will continue to feel this good and are disappointed when they don't. Then we get frustrated and think we must settle for unhappily ever after. I am here to show you how to get back to the romantic phase and make it even better!

Conflict

The next inevitable stage in any relationship is conflict. This stage can come and go at different times in relationships. This is the stage that will either make or break your relationship. Problems and differences of opinion will arise, and you will see the other person without those rose-colored glasses. Generally, men hope and assume their wives will stay just like they were during the romantic stage, and women hope and assume their husbands will change. This phase is easier for some people than others. Your family history and your past relationship experiences play a role in how you navigate this stage.

Remember, our families of origin are where we learn so much about being in a relationship. You learn either how to resolve conflicts and move on to the next stage or how to get stuck. If communication is poor and solutions aren't found, the relationship starts to deteriorate. This is when the love and passion can decline in your relationship. You might think this is a natural progression and just the way it is. You might not feel the need to make things better. Or you might try to improve things but fail and become even more frustrated, annoyed, disappointed, and resentful. Eventually, you may lose hope of having a better relationship. Sometimes relationships end at this point, or they continue unhappily ever after. Relationships fail for one of two reasons: either you are in the wrong relationship, or you haven't learned the skills to make it work. This book will give you the skills you need to move through this stage successfully, whether you are first entering this stage or have been stuck here for years. I will teach you how to break the patterns that are keeping you stuck, so you can move forward to the next stage, the unstoppable relationship.

Unstoppable Relationship

The ultimate goal of all relationships is to get to this stage, but sadly, too few ever do. An unstoppable relationship is one in which you and your partner are a team. You both see the relationship as a priority. This means spending time together consistently. Another element of the unstoppable stage is having open communication where problems are negotiated in a healthy manner and issues are resolved quickly. This also means speaking positively to and about each other and communicating regularly. Showing respect is another important part of this stage. Unconditional respect is essential to making our partners feel loved and wanted. Ultimately, respect breeds acceptance, which makes you and your partner feel closer to each other and allows for trust. Finally, the unstoppable stage has the above qualities plus the love and passion that you had at the beginning of the relationship. This aspect actually increases once you have reached this final stage. Will it feel the same as in the beginning? No, it will feel different, but I believe even better. You will experience that love and passion with the added benefits of respect, trust, love, friendship, security, vulnerability, and complete acceptance.

The first step in arriving at a new location is to know where you are going. It is important to have a vision of the relationship you desire.

Your Vision of the Future

Now that we have identified what an unstoppable relationship is and you have a better idea of what is possible, let's talk about how to get there. The first step in arriving at a new location is to know where you are going. So often when I talk to clients, they have no idea what their relationship visions are. They know they are frustrated or unsatisfied with the relationships they have, but they have no idea of what they really want. This is the first thing I address with all new clients who are married or single. It is important to have a vision of what you want for your relationship. Take some time to do an exercise now before you move forward in the book.

Exercise

Think about your ideal life with a partner. You are creating an ideal vision of a deeply satisfying love relationship. Spend some time just jotting down notes and thoughts about what your relationship would look and feel like. Imagine the life you want to live with your partner. What do you want to create and share in this relationship? How will you feel when you are in the relationship? How do you spend time together? How much time do you spend together daily, weekly, or monthly? You might also include ideas regarding family life, finances, friends, careers, spirituality, health, and hobbies.

Now that you have your notes, it is time to come up with a list or a written narrative of your life together. You can do both or just one, whichever feels more natural to you. Some people like to have lists, and others prefer a more free-flowing narrative. Whichever you decide to do, write it in the present tense as if it already exists. Also, write it with positive statements rather than what you do not want. Here are a few examples of statements:

- ♥ We laugh and have fun together.
- ♥ We trust each other.
- ♥ We communicate easily.
- ♥ We settle differences peacefully.
- ♥ We share private time together daily.
- ♥ We share similar parenting philosophies and are good parents.
- ♥ We have an active and satisfying sex life.

Now that you have your list or narrative, you can share it with your partner. You can even ask him to make a list of his own and compare your visions. This is an optional step, though, for the purpose of this book. I want you to keep this list close at hand and read it often. Perhaps take a moment each day to read it. Don't worry about making it perfect; it can change in time as your relationship progresses. The fundamentals will stay the same, though. It may be necessary to add or delete items as your life changes. If you are in a relationship, I want you to look at your list and see which items you already have and which could use some improvement. You will be able to see what areas need your time and attention. Don't get overwhelmed if there are too many areas that are not in line with your vision. This book will provide you with small steps you can take so that over time you can improve on all the areas and experience your vision of a deeply satisfying loving relationship.

Your relationship is your
safe haven at the end of the day.
It is the place you feel completely
loved for who you are.

Secret #1

Unstoppable Desire

Making Your Relationship a Safe Haven

The first step in creating an unstoppable relationship is
making it a priority and making sure your partner knows it! This
doesn't mean that the relationship is your only priority. That
isn't realistic. However, to feel loved and secure, you need to feel
like you and your partner are a team and that the relationship is
a top priority for both of you.

In order to be a team, I really believe that you need to have
the same core values and goals. Some of this gets worked out
in the conflict stage (described in the previous chapter). Once
you are clear on your shared core goals and values, the rest is
small stuff you can work on daily in order to have a fabulous

relationship. You both want to know that the other person is always there for you and that you can count on each other no matter what is going on in the outside world. Your relationship is your safe haven at the end of each day. It is the one place you feel completely loved for who you are.

Your partner wants and needs to feel like you are 100 percent committed to the relationship in order to feel safe and loved. So many times we start out doing a good job of communicating this to our partners, but then we get busy with children, work, and the demands of day-to-day life. We quit trying and think that our partners just know how we feel.

A gentleman once told me that he told his wife he loved her in the beginning of the relationship, and nothing had changed; he did not understand why he had to tell her again. He was making the assumption that she knew his feelings and didn't need to hear it again. In this case, his wife might not feel loved and appreciated causing her to withdraw her love and attention from her husband. She might feel dissatisfied and become emotionally distant and unhappy. This can begin to deteriorate the relationship.

Sometimes we quit trying and think that the relationship is just as good as it gets and really isn't even supposed to be any better. We simply stop putting in the extra effort. This can lead to a downward spiral in our relationships. When this happens, we start to get annoyed, frustrated, disappointed, and resentful of our partners. We start to focus on the negatives and behaviors we don't like. Women will question whether they are really loved, and men will not feel respected, which can lead to poor communication and loss of intimacy.

I know you have heard people in a group putting down their partners to others and complaining about them. Your focus shifts from all the things you love about your partner to all the things that you don't like. We will talk more about all of these areas later in the book, but for now, I just want you to be aware of what can happen when we forget to make our relationships a priority.

I have talked to so many individuals who told me they did not realize their marriages were in trouble until their partners asked for a divorce. Not all relationships end after years of arguing and fighting. Some couples just drift apart until they finally realize they are not getting their needs met in the current relationship and decide there may be more out there. The sad part is that a large percentage of these relationships could have been saved. The good news is that it only takes one person to transform a relationship.

If you feel your relationship is stoppable and do not feel like it is a priority for you or your partner, YOU have the power to turn this around. You can change your relationship by doing small things on a daily basis; that is the power of this book. It puts you in control, and it only takes small steps. When you show up differently in the relationship and begin to break unhealthy patterns, you can transform your relationship and create a better one.

Your partner needs to know that you are living as a team and nothing can come between you. You each are number one in the other's world. All humans have a need to feel secure and safe, and the place we should feel this is with our partners. This will lead to an increase in love and intimacy. When you feel safe and accepted by your partner, you are free to be truly yourself and create a closeness you have with no one else. It begins with you and some simple actions.

You see, when you start to make the relationship a priority by doing something on a daily basis, your partner will feel loved, accepted, safe, and cherished by you. He will know that he has top billing in your life! When he feels this way, he will start to act differently toward you! It may take some time, and the progress may be slow in some relationships, but you will notice changes. I have had some clients tell me how amazed they were that changing one small behavior led to noticeable differences in how their partners treated them. You can't control your partner's actions, and trying to will only create more conflict in the relationship. The better approach is to be proactive: make yourself a better partner. When you do this with the intention of really wanting to show your partner how much you love and care for him, he will *feel* loved and cared for. This will lead him to change his feelings toward you. I know sometimes you would rather your partner be the one to make the first move and change first, but remember the vision activity you did earlier. Keep in mind that it all starts with what you want for your relationship. This is where you are headed, and you are on the road to get there.

So what are some small things you can start to do today to make your relationship a priority? Do something every day. It can be something small. Vary what you do. Use words and actions to show your partner how much he means to you.

Remember when you were first dating? What things did you do then to attract him? Go back to doing those things. What have you done in the past that got a good reaction from your partner? Do more of that. If you are still not sure what to do, ask him. He will tell you what makes him feel loved and cherished. It is different for each person. Some people prefer physical acts, and some prefer words. If you do some of both, he is sure to get the message. I will give you some suggestions, but I really encourage you to come up with your own ideas. I also encourage you to be on the lookout for opportunities that arise to compliment your partner or to tell him how much you appreciate something he has done. Sometimes it may be simply telling him that you love him. Throughout this book you will be getting more ideas of how to do this, but for now here are a few suggestions to get you started.

1. **Be present.** Don't take your partner for granted. Be present in his life. This means being emotionally present not just physically present. Take time to ask about things that are important to him. Show an active interest in his life.

2. **Encourage him.** Taking an interest is the first step, but don't stop there. Give him advice when appropriate, but always give the gift of your support and encouragement.

3. **Be more affectionate.** Hug and kiss more. Hold hands or give a back rub. Find opportunities and ways to increase your show of physical affection. We will talk more about why this is so important in the Secret #4 chapter.

4. **Set aside time.** Set aside some time daily for your partner. I know you are busy, but find a small amount of

time for your partner each day. Check in with him to see how his day went. Talk about issues you need to deal with. Relax and enjoy each other's company. You get the idea! It doesn't matter as much what you do as long as you give the gift of your undivided attention.

5. **Practice niceties.** Keep niceties in the relationship. Just as we teach our children to say please and thank you, remember to ask kindly and address the other person in a loving and respectful way. Examples might include the following: a warm greeting in the morning, asking how his day was, saying please and thank you, etc.

These are just a few ideas, but I am sure you can come up with a whole list of your own. The important thing is not so much what you do but that you do something consistently. Make it something your partner will appreciate, and watch what happens to your relationship.

Exercise

Make a list of things you can do to show your partner how much you appreciate him. Add to your list as you come up with new ideas. Take note of what your partner likes and change or add to your list accordingly. Try to do something daily.

Pathway to Happiness

In an unstoppable relationship, you will remember more good times than bad and will work on creating those experiences and those memories. You will not take the relationship for granted but will be willing to put in time and effort to keep the relationship fresh and exciting. We pursue our partners in the beginning of our relationships and spend lots of time and effort letting them know how much we want them and how much they mean to us. Then we get married and give them less time and attention! Have you ever considered doing more once you are married and not less? It is so important to let your partner know how much he means to you and how much you appreciate him. I know this sounds simple, but we forget to do it. When was the last time you not only told your partner how much you love and appreciate him but also flirted with him? You remember how playful you were when you were dating? It was lots of fun! It is important to continue to court your partner throughout the relationship; don't become complacent. The little things really do matter!

Sometime after we have been in our relationships for a period of time, they begin to get stale, and the excitement is gone. When those rose-colored glasses we were wearing in the romantic phase come off, we find ourselves wondering who are we in these relationships with. Sometimes they do not resemble the partners we started with. This does not mean they necessarily changed; we may just be seeing them from different vantage points. Little things start to annoy us, and we focus more on the negatives. We get caught up in the day-to-day frustrations of sharing our lives with someone. Small things begin to bother us that had not before. If you are focusing on all the things you do not like about your partner, you will notice those more often, and it will change the way you feel about the other person. You will become more frustrated, critical, and unhappy in the relationship. Have you gotten in the habit of taking your partner for granted? Do you focus on the things you don't like about your partner and criticize him? Frequently couples get in the habit of telling each other everything they do wrong or what they want the other to do differently.

How often do you tell your partner what he did right? How often do you praise him and show gratitude for all he does for you? How often do you tell him that you love them? It is easy to assume that our partners know how we feel. We believe that because there are no disagreements, all is well. We stop expressing our love and forget to show gratitude to the people we share our lives with. You hear others complaining about their partners, and you start to complain about yours. These habits are easy to get into, but they are detrimental to your relationship. The good news is that if it is easy to get into bad habits, why not get into good habits that will support and deepen your relationship? Small steps taken on a daily basis will become habits, and the love and intimacy will return and grow. Habits of love and appreciation and gratitude are just as easy to foster as habits of criticism and resentment. Remember when we focus on one negative, we miss five positives.

What you need sometimes at this stage in the relationship is a new perspective. It is time to remember all the reasons you fell in love and chose this person to be your mate in the first place. Shift your perspective to one of gratitude and appreciation. Acceptance and respect for the other is crucial. Learning to accept him for who he is without trying to change him is important. This change in perspective requires you to look at the big picture in your relationship and to focus on the relationship as a whole and not on the little details. You develop a mindset that you and your partner are a team. When deciding how to respond to your partner, always keep in mind the end result you are going for: an unstoppable relationship! Will your attitude and actions help or hurt your relationship?

I talk to clients about finding perfection in imperfection. In my house, I am very neat and like things to be where they belong. I am very visual and like my surroundings to look as perfect as possible. I have children who do not feel the same way. They seem perfectly happy to have their stuff all around them in no particular order. My guy likes things to be clean in the house, but he is not always as neat as I am. He is not a messy person by any means; he just isn't as perfectionistic as I am. Few people are.

I have a choice to make every day. I can let small things bother me and think why can't he just pick that up and put it away, or I can find the perfection in the situation. I can smile and be thankful that he is in my life! I can appreciate him for who he is without trying to change him. Now if mess starts accumulating around the house, I would have to discuss this with him. We might need to compromise and find a way for us both to live happily in one house. Instead, I look around the house and feel appreciative that he is considerate enough of my wishes to help me keep the house neat. My children on the other hand are not of that age just yet, and they have to be reminded to keep their piles picked up and contained. Even then, I look at their messes and usually am able to smile and appreciate them being in my life at this age. It will not last very long, and I will be begging them to come out of their rooms and spend time with me! I think we find this change in perspective easier to do with our children than with our partners.

You need to realize that the other person is not you. If you expect him to think and act like you, you will be disappointed and frustrated. He has his own history and beliefs and ways of thinking and doing things. He will not always act the way you think he should. It is important to ask yourself why his behavior is bothering you. Sometimes it really isn't all about him at all. We are responsible for our own happiness and no one else's, but there are times when we blame someone else, especially our significant others for our unhappiness. This is easier than taking a look at our own stuff and dealing with what is really bothering us.

Albert Schweitzer once said, "Success is not the key to happiness. Happiness is the key to success." The science of happiness is actually taught and studied at Harvard University, among other places. Too often we think that if certain areas of our lives (relationships being among the major ones) were just in order, we would be happy. The research actually says the opposite. It is important to realize that we are responsible for our own happiness.

Show your partner love and respect on a daily basis. Accept him for who he is and remember why you chose him in the first place. I suggest you start creating positive moments for yourself and your partner. Write down things daily that you like about your partner or things he did that you liked. Try to come up with a different one each day. Don't just repeat the same ones. This will start to train your mind to focus on the positive, and your emotions will follow suit. It will become a habit to notice all the good about him. Ask yourself, "What do I love about him? What do I like? What do I respect? What did he do that I appreciate?" I would suggest that you pick at least one of those things each day to share with your partner.

If you do this for a period of time, you will be amazed at how your thoughts about your partner change. I would suggest making this a priority and keeping a journal for the next ninety days. Make it a point to jot down something at the end of each day. You will notice more things about him that you like and more reasons to love him. When you are treating him with this much love and respect, you will start to get more in return. His love for you will increase as well. You will also notice that you are happier! How can you not be happier when your focus is on all the things you like instead of dislike?

Ladies, men fall in love and stay in love based on how they feel when they are with you. Try and focus on being positive and pleasant to be around. It really is about the small things such as the small, caring gestures, the heartfelt smile, the random act of kindness, or showing interest in your partner's day. Take an active interest in your partner and see what happens. These are just the tip of the iceberg, and I know you can think of many more examples. Keep a positive attitude and do these things daily to improve your relationship.

The good news is it only takes one person to transform a

relationship. You can show up differently in the relationship and begin to break unhealthy patterns.

Exercise

Create a list of things you like and appreciate about your partner. Try to come up with a different one each day and share this with your partner.

- ♥ What do you love about him?
- ♥ What do you like?
- ♥ What do you respect?
- ♥ What did he do that you appreciate?

Random Acts Of Kindness

We make choices every day, all day. These choices, if repeated over and over again, become habits. The choices that we make and the habits that we form have a great deal of power in our lives. These seemingly small things done over and over again make a big difference in our lives and in our relationships. My goal in this book is to break down the keys to creating an unstoppable relationship into small, easy-to-follow tips. These small but powerful choices and actions are what make the difference between having an unsatisfactory relationship or having one full of love and passion!

Have you gotten in the habit of taking your partner for granted? We get busy with life, and our relationships take a back seat. They are no longer our top priorities, and we tend to function on autopilot. We just talked about how important it is for partners to feel like part of a team and a priority. This is essential to the happiness of our relationships. Why not get into habits that will support and deepen our partnerships? Small steps taken on a daily basis will become habits that will nurture our bonds. Habits of love and appreciation and gratitude are just as easy to foster as habits of criticism and resentment. Find ways to show love, appreciation, and gratitude, and to show random acts of kindness toward your partner. Show love and respect on a daily basis. What can you do today and every day to build your relationship up? Here are just a few ideas to get you started.

1. **Say thank you.** Compliment and praise your partner. Be appreciative and say thank you for all the things he does for you. Do this when you are talking to him or maybe leave a note somewhere he can find it. Do this in front of him and make sure to do it in front of others. Show him how proud you are of him. Try to keep this timely and recognize something he has done recently. Your partner will feel appreciated, and you will find that by paying attention to these things, you appreciate your partner more!

2. **Have fun and be playful.** Sometimes we take life too seriously. What can you do to add more fun to your relationship? It can be something as simple as finding something to laugh about together, dancing in the living room just for fun, watching a funny movie, or anything that is light and playful. Maybe it can even be playful and sexy.

3. **Surprise him with something small.** For no reason at all except you love and appreciate him, do something nice for him as a surprise. Maybe bring home a movie he likes,

make a favorite dinner or go out to dinner, or bring your partner a card—anything small that he would like. This can be a gift or just time spent with you doing something he likes.

4. **Text.** Randomly send your partner a text telling him how much you love him, how much he means to you, that you are thinking of him, or that you would choose him as your partner again. Send flirty, playful texts, or share an inside joke—anything that will let him know how important he is to you and that you are thinking of him. This is a great way to connect.

5. **Give him the gift of you.** Yes, I am talking about sex. Physical intimacy is essential to a good relationship and is a great way to show your partner how much you love him. We will discuss this at length later in the book. The connection you share during lovemaking is unlike any other bond. Start with an extra hug and kiss in the morning, and tell your partner how nice he looks; send hints throughout the day. Build the anticipation. Then enjoy reconnecting.

Exercise

What random act of kindness can you do today for your partner to show him how much you care and how important he is to you? It can be something small that you do, but those small things add up to help you create an unstoppable relationship! Start a list that you can add to and pick something daily.

" *When you leave the room to go to the kitchen to get something for yourself, ask you partner if they need anything. Little acts of kindness go a long way.*
Always give a kiss and say goodbye when you are leaving home; it could by your last kiss.
Don't get historical when disagreements arise.
You cannot change the past. You are living in today. Tomorrow is not guaranteed. **"**

- Nancy W.

" *We are very clear with each other that we are totally committed to one another for life. I completely trust that my wife has my back. I would feel very sorry for anyone that ever disparages me in front of her.*
We practice being "interested" with one another vs. being "interesting" to one another. **"**

- Rob F.

" *It was about marrying your best friend. He is the person you first think of when you have exciting news or person you go to, to lean on. If you aren't the best friends first, it's a long haul ahead.* **"**

- Patty S.

" *My husband and I have been a couple for twenty-eight* *years, married for twenty-three. A topic that's come up quite regularly that we feel strongly about in maintaining a healthy relationship is for both partners to put 100 percent into the relationship. You'll hear many say "a relationship is 50/50," but that's only putting in half the effort, and that's where issues arise. Where in life did we learn that 50 percent effort was good enough? Each party to the relationship must always put 100 percent of themselves into preserving and growing the marriage. There certainly will be times when one partner has to carry a heavier burden; however, that doesn't mean that both aren't putting in all the effort they can at any given time. When you put in 100 percent, you are valuing your partner and your marriage. It is in this way that we as a couple have matured and grown, by consistently understanding that we are doing the best we can and not blaming each other for struggles we may encounter as life happens. Knowing that we are each committed to having the best marriage possible, when a stumbling block arises, we make the time to discuss it. We don't play the blame game, and we have faith that whatever decisions we make are for the good of our marriage and for the good of our family. Therefore, when we deal with issues that do arise, our partner's state of mind is never in question. It allows us to deal quickly with the problem at hand without getting stuck in an unending circle of blame.* 🙶

- Renee H.

It is really about the small
things such as small gestures,
the heartfelt smile, or
random acts of kindness.

When we understand our partners
better, how they think and
what they need in relationships,
it is much easier to appreciate the
differences and navigate the road
to those unstoppable relationships.

Secret #2

Unstoppable Understanding

Men and Women: We Are Different

Men and women are different! I am sure this comes as no surprise to you. Just how different and why we are different may surprise you! We know we act and think differently; yet, we still get frustrated with each other and sometimes angry with our partners because they do not act like we expect or want them to. We may be frustrated because we can't figure out what to do to make them happy, and we don't understand what we are doing wrong. Women tend to feel unloved when they are misunderstood, and men feel disrespected. It is important to realize that men and women need different things in a relationship. The differences between men and women are important because this is what creates the attraction and the passion.

The key is to understand each other and learn to appreciate and cherish the differences in order to have a happier relationship. It is important that you break the cycle of blame and stop trying to find fault with your partner. Remember that you are a team. Appreciate instead of criticize.

There are lots of ways in which men and women are different that affect our relationships. As children, we learn that girls can do anything boys can do and that boys may show their feminine sides. There certainly isn't anything wrong with that; however, what we don't learn is that there are actual physical differences in brain structure and development that affect how boys and girls think and communicate. No wonder we are frustrated with each other! This section will cover a wide variety of ideas to help you understand your partner better, and you will use this knowledge throughout the remainder of the book. We have already discussed that making the relationship a priority and acting as a team is essential for a satisfying relationship. When we understand our partners better, how they think and what they need in relationships, it is so much easier to appreciate the differences and navigate the road to those unstoppable relationships.

Scientific Evidence

First, let's look at some of the scientific research that explains the differences in men's and women's brains. The male and female brains show differences even in utero. They are washed with hormones that start the process by which our brains develop male and female tendencies. The male brain is washed with testosterone, which affects its development. This testosterone drives the assertive, problem solving, and competitive characteristics of men. From an evolutionary standpoint, men are programmed to be less social and to compete in order to reproduce and pass on their genes. They do not look for connections the way women do. The female brain is washed in estrogen, which leads to more social behavior, more emotions, and more language skills. From an evolutionary standpoint, women banded together for safety and to raise children. They learned to communicate as a way to stay safe and connected.

As far as the brain itself is concerned, there are physical differences as well. Men have a larger amygdala, which is influenced by hormones and, in male brains, has testosterone receptors that heighten responses. This part of the brain helps men process fear, triggers aggression, and stimulates competiveness. Men and women respond very differently to the amygdala's "fight or flight" signal. Men tend to withdraw socially and move toward action; whereas, women tend to seek connections as they find comfort in groups. Another area of the brain, the corpus callosum, the part of the brain that connects the two hemispheres, is thicker in women enabling them to use both sides of the brain at the same time. The testosterone wash that occurs in male fetuses actually dissolves portions of the connections. On the other hand, the estrogen in the female brain actually prompts the nerve cells to grow more connections between the hemispheres. This could explain why men use the right side of the brain for spatial skills and the left for verbal, whereas women use both sides simultaneously. This may also explain why men are more able to compartmentalize areas of life and focus on one thing at a time, while women tend to connect everything. You may have heard the analogy that men's brains are like waffles and women's are like spaghetti. Much like the "boxes" of a waffle, men tend to compartmentalize life and put events and ideas into separate spaces, or in other words they think of one thing at a time. They also tend to deal with one issue at a time. This ability to compartmentalize makes them good at problem solving.

Women's brains are more like spaghetti. All areas of our lives are mixed up together and connected. Every issue and thought is connected to every other thought and issue, which is why women are said to be better at multitasking. We move from thought to thought easily. This is where frustration can enter in a relationship. Men are actually capable of thinking of nothing, and women do not understand that. When a woman asks her partner what he is thinking about, and he says, "Nothing," she assumes he is keeping something from her. In actuality, he may be simply focusing on the task at hand, whether it's watching football or reading a book. With spaghetti brains, that is much harder for women to do. We have a hard time shutting down our thoughts. This is where communication between men and women could get complicated. Women are jumping from topic to topic and connecting different areas, and men tend to focus on one task at a time. We will discuss this in more detail in the section on communication. For now, I just want you to understand that we are different, and we are not being different to agitate the other person or to be difficult. Our brains truly are hardwired that way. It is important that we learn to understand more about how our partners think and what they need in a relationship, so we can move forward.

Get the Love You Want and Become Irresistible to Him

Remember when you were first together, and he couldn't get enough of you? Remember how good it felt to know he wanted only you and was in love with you? The beginning of a relationship is wonderful with all the chemistry flowing and those "feel good" hormones racing through your body. Eventually though, we make it past the romantic love stage and have to learn how to continue getting the love we want and being irresistible to him! In long-term relationships, we are more in love with our partners at times and less in love with them at other times. In order to have an unstoppable relationship, we must work to keep the love alive. The most important thing for women in a relationship is to feel unconditional love. Women are fundamentally insecure when it comes to feeling loved. Even if we have a good relationship and feel secure, we still need and want reassurance. Remember the story of the man who told his wife he loved her once and did not think he had to say it again because nothing had changed? Even when we know logically that nothing has changed, we still need to hear it and feel it often.

I am a relationship specialist, and I still find myself feeling insecure. I have learned that when I am not happy with my relationship at the moment, I need to take a look at what is really going on. Just stopping and asking myself what I am upset about is the first step. I try to do this before I say anything to anyone else. The times when I don't do this and immediately act on my feelings, communication breaks down and feelings can get hurt. I realize afterward that a negative situation could have been avoided if I had only taken some time to analyze my feelings and act on the real issue. I frequently find a feeling of not being a priority is what's really underneath, which is really about not feeling loved. Now if I take this one step further, I may just find that my guy has done nothing wrong; he cannot read my mind after all. He doesn't know that I am feeling insecure. His feelings have not changed, so how could he know. I need to realize I am feeling insecure and need some reassurance. Instead of being upset with him or telling him what he did wrong, I find a way to get my needs met. I find it is really pretty easy to feel loved again if I just look at the positives, like we talked about in a previous chapter. What did he do today that showed me he loves me? Remember that we all feel loved in different ways. Maybe he did something that means love to him but may not be something I recognize as love.

I hear this frequently from clients. Our partners are more likely to show us love in the same way they feel loved. Now if you prefer other forms, it is okay to share some ideas with your partner on how you feel loved, but I would suggest you do this in a positive manner. Tell your partner want you DO want instead of what you don't want. Remember to always let him know what he is doing right. This will make him feel successful, and he will want to do more of it. Our guys really do want to please us, especially if they feel appreciated. Remember that men compartmentalize in boxes and will spend time in the boxes they feel they are successful. They will seek out the boxes that work and ignore those that confuse them or make them feel like failures. The key to understand here is that men strive to be successful at everything. If they feel like they may not succeed, they tend to stay away from it. This can mean their relationships. A man will lose interest and quit trying if he feels he cannot please you. A man will not stay in love if he is not appreciated.

So let him know what he is doing right and give some suggestions on what else he could do to show his love. Men are not mind readers and do not always know what makes us happy. Sometimes it is just our need for more reassurance and unconditional love. The more you can accept love in different ways, the more loved you will feel. Women thrive on attention from their guys. Remember that we need to feel like we are a priority and that the relationship comes before anything else. When you are not feeling like a priority, what can you do that will bring about the result you want?

First, you need to understand what you need from your partner. We just talked about needing unconditional love and reassurance of it often. We also need loyalty from our partners. This comes with feeling like we are loved and a priority. We want to feel like they would choose us all over again. We want to feel loved and cherished and beautiful. We need to feel emotionally connected to our partners. We want to be pursued and dated just like when we were first together. Women need more attention generally than men do. If you are not getting this in your relationship, it might be time to initiate some of it yourself. I know—most women would prefer that the man do the initiating, but keep in mind that people are attracted to partners who are responsible for their own happiness. We can suggest ideas to our partners, and for some couples this works really well. For others, they need to take the initiative in the beginning. The end result is what you are after. If you can put aside how the experience started and just enjoy it, you will gain so much. Create moments together that give you what you desire and also create moments that he enjoys. Let him know how much those moments mean to you and how happy they make you, and watch him start to initiate more of them in the future. Ultimately, though, it is the experience and the feeling of being loved that you are after, not how you got there. Remember that he wants to succeed, so set up situations where you both feel loved and appreciated.

Something else that is very important for couples is a date night. What you do is not as important as the spending time together. Plan within your budget, and if you have children, then plan around them. Go out if you can and recreate fun dates you had in the beginning of your relationship. Take a walk, watch favorite TV shows together, snuggle and talk at the end of the day, exercise together, cook together, or anything else that you share and look forward to. It is important to make this time fun and enjoyable for both of you. Men are attracted to our happiness and our positive emotions. If you find yourself complaining or being negative during your time together, this will be a turn off to your guy. He will not want to give you the attention you desire. I know things happen in life, and we cannot always be in a good mood. That is not realistic. But men like us to be playful, and this is something we frequently lose in our time together. Make sure you are incorporating fun and playfulness in your date nights or special time together. Men want to be in love and to be happy with you. Adding some intimacy in the mix is always a positive. More on that topic later!

It is also important for women to reconnect with their guys at the end of the day. We want his undivided attention and to feel connected after being apart. We want to feel heard. The problem that frequently arises here is that women are more verbal than men, and we often overwhelm him with information and emotions as soon as he walks in the door. Then we feel unloved when we do not get the responses we desire or need. Here is where we need to understand the differences between men and women to solve this problem. Remember that your guy was initially attracted to you by the way he felt when he was around you. He prefers less drama and likes things to be more on an even keel. Consider how you are approaching him when he comes home. Do you begin complaining and bombarding him the moment he walks through the door? This can make a big difference in the response you get.

During my marriage, I would take time to freshen up and maybe even change my clothes, so I looked and felt attractive before my husband came home. Physical connection is very important to me, so I was usually ready with a big hug and kiss for him. What I neglected to do some days was to give him time to unwind before I started dumping my stuff on him. I would want to tell him all about my day the second he came home. This may overwhelm some men.

Let's go back to the male brain and its compartments. He may still be focused on work when he first gets home, or he may be burned out from work and need some down time. He may need some time to process the day before transitioning to family life. It is not that he does not care about your day or care about the family. It is just not the right time. You would get more of what you wanted and needed if you could give him some time to change clothes, hug the kids, eat dinner, and unwind in some way before you expect his undivided attention to deal with your day. This is one of those instances where understanding your guy and working with the differences will benefit you and your relationship.

I encourage you to try something different for yourself. When you first reconnect after being apart, try initiating physical contact. I am not just talking about a quick hug and a kiss on the cheek that has no meaning. I am talking about a warm loving hug and a big kiss that shows you missed him. You can take this one step further and start by texting him before he gets home to let him know you missed him and are looking forward to seeing him. Then allow him to adjust to being home in whatever way he needs. Allow him his space to move from one compartment in his brain to the next. Then pick a time when he is able to give you his undivided attention, even if it is briefly, and share your day with him. If you make this a positive experience for him, he will respond more positively, and you will both get what you want and need. That is the ultimate goal here after all.

There is nothing like the feeling of being in love and having butterflies in your stomach when you see your partner. It does take work in a relationship to keep those feelings alive, but it can be done, and it is so worth the effort. I want you to get up every morning feeling excited to be sharing your life with such a wonderful partner. The more you understand, appreciate, and love him, the more he will appreciate and love you. You will get the love you desire, and you will become irresistible to him.

Exercises

Take a moment now to think about what you have learned from this chapter. What insights did you have? You might need to reread it and take notes as you go.

- ♥ What did you learn about yourself?
- ♥ What did you learn about your partner?
- ♥ What did you learn about your relationship?
- ♥ What can you do differently in your relationship to utilize the information?

Make a list of how you feel loved. Include all the things you would like your partner to do on one side, and on the other side, list all the things he does to show you love. You can use this to give him ideas of things he can do. Just make sure you approach this in a positive way. I also want you to look at the list of what he is doing, even if it is not what you want him to do. It is important to acknowledge what he is doing right. Be sure to thank him for all he does. This will make him feel appreciated, and he will be more willing to do some of the things on your list that he might not have thought of.

Next time you are feeling upset with something your partner has done or maybe not done, stop before you say anything. Do something to calm down, maybe take a walk, a bath, or anything that takes your mind off being upset. Once you are feeling better, ask yourself what is really upsetting you? Is it really the event or is there an underlying issue? If so, deal with the underlying issue and not the actual event. Look for patterns that might need to be addressed.

Make Him Feel Like Superman

We all want to feel loved in our relationships, but how we feel loved is different for men and women. Often, people show love in the way they feel love and not the way their partners need love. We just talked about how important it is for women to feel unconditionally loved in their relationship. For men, love and respect are synonymous. The most important aspect of a relationship for them is unconditional respect. This is more important than feeling loved. Men would rather feel unloved than disrespected. They assume you love them, but frequently, they do not feel respected by their partners. This is something a lot of women do not know, and it is essential to creating an unstoppable relationship. By showing your man respect, you are actually showing him love in the way he needs it most. When he feels respected by you, he is more motivated to show you love because he is feeling more in love with you! Do you want to know how to make your guy feel like Superman in your relationship?

Admire and Appreciate

It is important to let men know how much you admire and appreciate them and all they do for our families and us. In the last chapter, we talked about men losing interest in relationships if they feel they cannot please us. They will quit trying, and then we feel unloved. The more we feel unloved, the more we stop appreciating them. It is a vicious cycle that needs to be broken. Remember—he really does want to please you. He wants to be successful in all areas of his life, including his relationship, and he really does want to love you. He may not know how to show you, and he may have stopped trying if he has consistently failed or if you have failed to acknowledge his efforts. If what he hears most are complaints and criticism, he will quit trying, and his feelings will begin to change. A man will not stay in love if he is not appreciated. How often do you acknowledge all your guy does for you?

Do you tell him how much you appreciate his going to work every day to provide for the family, even if you work as well? It is important for men to feel like they are appreciated for providing for the family. I talk to a lot of women who stay home with the children all day. By the time their husbands come home, the women are really ready for a break. I have stayed home all day with children myself and completely understand the need for a break at the end of the day. What sometimes happens though is that the women act angry with their husbands and communicate their need for a break in a very negative way. They do not sound like team players, and the poor husbands are bombarded with negativity as soon as they get home.

There are two reasons why this causes problems in a relationship. First, remember that he compartmentalizes and may not be out of the work compartment in his brain. He may need time to get into the family compartment. Secondly, he has been working hard all day to provide and will see this behavior as disrespect for all he is doing. This may cause him to withdraw and be less likely to want to help with the family. By understanding men and appreciating the differences, you can get a better outcome for yourself and your relationship. I am here to help you get the love you want while giving him the respect he wants. It really is a win/win situation.

Let's take this same situation and see what you can do differently. If you've been home all day with the kids, take a few minutes to freshen up before he walks in the door. After all, if you stay at home or work from home, you probably rolled out of bed and went straight to work. You might have been in your pajamas all day or have Cheerios stuck in your hair. You may not feel very feminine or attractive. You have been doing for others all day long, so take some time to do for yourself. Freshen up mentally as well as physically to embrace all your relationship has to offer. If you've been away at work all day, spend some time on the drive home thinking positive thoughts about your partner and anticipating reconnecting. Be proactive in switching gears from work to home. Then greet him with all the love you feel for him. Give him a hug and kiss and welcome him home. Men are looking for a soft place to land at the end of the day. That is very important to them. The world can be tough on all of us, and we want our partners to be our support systems. Maybe ask him how his day was. Give him a few minutes to switch gears if he needs that. Let him know how much you appreciate his working so hard for the family. Now he will feel loved and respected. He will be much more likely to respond in a positive way if you ask him nicely to help with the children or the dishes or whatever else you need. He will also be more open to hearing about your day. This is how you work as a team and utilize the differences in order to create a better relationship. This will go a long way toward making him feel like Superman. This is just one example of how you can show him appreciation. What other ways can you think of?

Respect Differences

We know men and women are different, and we have talked some about why. Now it is important to learn to appreciate those differences instead of expecting him to think and act like you. Men feel close to us when we love and accept them for who they are instead of trying to change them. We show respect when we allow them to be men. We also want them to do the same for us. We want to be accepted for being women. We are initially attracted to each other because of these differences, so now is the time to respect them. One way we can do this is by allowing them time to be guys. Encourage your partner to spend time with his friends or to spend time on his favorite hobby. Keep in mind that it is just as important that we have separate interests and our own identities. We need time to connect with other females where we can talk, share emotions, and do things he is not interested in. Guys need time to bond with other men. Then when we come back together, we are refreshed and ready to spend quality time together as a couple. Try to remember this the next time you become critical of him and his need to be a guy. Changing your perception and your attitude will go a long way in how he feels about you and your relationship. Remember what you have learned in this book and realize he is acting and thinking differently because of how his brain really is hardwired. He will fall in love with you all over again as he feels safe and secure being himself. He will feel that you love and respect him unconditionally. This is the same kind of love we give our children but forget to give our partners sometimes. We are unique individuals, and this isn't about being the same but about being a team.

Trust His Judgment

We show respect for men when we trust their judgment, opinions, decisions, and knowledge. This does not mean we are not equally as smart or capable. It is important to let your guy know that you are asking for his input, seriously weighing it, and appreciative of his help. It is critical not to argue and question his decisions all the time. This is a very touchy subject for men. They need to know we trust them, need them, and value their opinions. Sometimes it is more important to defer to them, remembering that you are a team and that he needs to feel appreciated in this way. So ask for his advice, and make sure you let him know you appreciate his input. Take some time to give thought to his ideas before you make a decision. He might have another point of view that is helpful, or it might just be more important to defer to him for the sake of the relationship. Even if you decide not to take his advice, make sure he knows you appreciate his input. He will feel needed and respected and love you for it.

Trust His Abilities

As women, we show our caring and support by offering to help each other. If we ask a friend if she needs help in the kitchen and she says no, we might help her anyway because we know she really could use the help but just doesn't want to bother us. At least we will stay there and talk to her while she works. This is one way women bond. Men on the other hand are very different. If we ask our guy if he needs help with a project and he says no, he means it. When we insist on helping him anyway, he feels like we distrust him or do not think he is capable. For example, when he is installing the new TV system, allow him to do it his way and in his own time. It is ok to ask if he would like some help, but when he says no, respect that. I would even prefer for you to tell him that you trust he will ask for your assistance if he wants it. Let him know you are available, but that is all. Some men will enjoy doing projects together if they can take the lead, but others prefer to do it alone. Here is another time to respect the differences and not criticize his way of doing things, even if you feel your way is better. It is about the relationship and not about being right. Knowing how important this is to a guy helps us to respond in a respectful way, and again he will love and respect you for it.

Encouraging Success

I hear women complain frequently that their partners aren't helping enough around the house. Here is a cycle we can get into that frustrates both partners. When we constantly criticize our guy, we don't give him a chance to succeed, and this may come off as disrespectful in his eyes. When we criticize, he may feel a lack of trust, and eventually, he quits trying. He may become frustrated enough to let you take over and stop offering to help at all. Then we get more frustrated because he isn't doing what we want. It deteriorates the relationship. We are not showing him respect, and he doesn't feel as in love with us. It is important to ask him for help, but remember that he needs to do it in his own time and in his own way. Let him know you have confidence and faith in his ability, even if he does things differently. Let's get back to trusting him and allowing him to be the guy. Your partner will be happier with you, and ultimately, you will be happier with him.

A lot of times we contribute to our own frustrations because we expect him to do it our way; we criticize how he is doing it, and we criticize the time frame he is doing it in. I do understand that the trash has to go out in time for trash day, and that may be something you need to discuss if it is not happening. Ultimately, you must let your partner know you trust in his ability. Appreciating him after he has done something will go a long way in making your guy feel loved and respected. Then you will feel better about the relationship, and you will feel better about him. Perhaps you won't be as overwhelmed because you are getting more help, and your relationship will be more about support and gratitude rather than criticism and frustration.

For me personally, I choose men who do things in a different time frame than I do. I tend to be attracted to guys who are more laid back by nature. I tend to be higher strung. I think there are many advantages to these differences, and I think I have chosen wisely. I need their more relaxed nature to balance me and calm me down. When my guy does things in a different way or different time frame than I would, I have a choice. I can get upset and criticize, or I can realize I chose him for who he is and remember all the good his unique personality brings to the relationship. I have a choice in my attitude and actions. Choosing to respect the differences and appreciate them builds my relationship instead of tearing it down. Do I always get my way? Do I always get things done exactly when and how I want? No! But I am perfectly happy with my guy and our relationship. I love and appreciate him the way he is!

Respect in Communication

Communication is the next key to an unstoppable relationship, and we will go into more detail later, but for now, let's look at how we show respect in communication. We do this by listening to him. Show interest in his day and the things that are important to him. We have already discussed the importance of allowing him to give his advice and opinions and really listening to them. Remember not to criticize or be overly negative or dramatic in your communication. Men hear criticism as disrespect and will shut down. Men really are more sensitive than we think, and when they get their feelings hurt, it can take them longer to get over it. They tend to show this in a different way than women do. We get angry or upset and voice our hurt, whereas men are more likely to shut down and pull away from the relationship. We all have different personalities, so this may look a little different depending on the individual, but it is good general knowledge to help us understand our guys. Again, remember to tell him you are proud of him and to let him know what he is doing right in the relationship!

Showing respect in public is another very important issue for men. It is important to always show your guy respect in public. Never put him down or criticize him around others, even when he isn't with you. You are a team, and he needs to know he can count on you. It can be easy to forget this if others around you are complaining about their partners, but it is detrimental to the relationship. Not only will he be very hurt by this behavior, but it will also affect how you see him. When you focus on the negative, you feel more disconnected and are more easily annoyed. It is important to focus on what you like and appreciate, and then remember to tell him. This goes back to the exercise I had you do in the beginning of the book where you listed all the things you liked about your partner, why you picked him in the first place.

When he feels respected, he feels loved. When he feels loved, he will feel more in love with you and will show you more of the love you desire. The more you show him respect, the more positive your attitude about him will become, the more you will feel like you are a team, and the better your communication will become. All of this will lead to more love and passion in your life and more happiness and contentment in your relationship. Step by step, we are leading you down the path to that vision of the relationship you wrote about—that unstoppable relationship!

Exercise

Go back now and look at the different ways to show respect we talked about in this chapter. In which areas are you doing a great job? Which areas could use some improvement? Take some time to journal about past events or conversations that did not go well and make notes about how you could have handled the situation in a different way.

How do you show your guy respect? What can you add to that list after reading this chapter? Pick one to try and see what his reaction is. Keep adding to that list and watch your relationship change for the better.

Unleash Your Feminine Energy and Reclaim Passion

At our cores, we all have a predominate energy that is either masculine or feminine. Generally, women have feminine core energy, and men have masculine core energy. This energy plays a major role in our lives and our relationships. Let's talk about what it means to have masculine and feminine energy and why it is important to our relationships.

Masculine energy is all about action, doing, thinking, giving, decision-making, analyzing, leading, and problem solving. Masculine energy is all about action and being assertive. Some examples of acting in masculine energy are making lists, giving advice, and accomplishing tasks.

Feminine energy is more about just being, feeling, expressing, intuiting, following, receiving, and being vulnerable and open. Feminine energy tends toward long walks, conversation, candles, perfume, softness, and music. Feminine energy is more about being in the moment instead of doing.

In day-to-day life, men and women act in both masculine and feminine ways. We all have both of these energies inside us and need to utilize both in order to function in life. Depending on our jobs, we may tap into more of one than the other. We may choose our jobs based on how in-tune we are to this energy. During most of the day, it is all about balancing these two energies and using them to our advantage to accomplish what we need to do that day. However, our masculine and feminine energy play an important role in our relationships as well. Understanding how we use this energy is one of the key factors in making a successful relationship and will be the focus for this section. It is this difference in energy that causes the attraction between men and women in relationships, and we want to use this to our advantage with our partners.

Men generally have masculine core energy, and that same energy is generally what they use a lot of at work. When they come home, they can stay in that energy in their relationship. It might need to look a little different when they are interacting with their partners, but the core energy will be the same. Women, on the other hand, spend a great deal of time functioning in masculine energy. It is part of the role we now play in society and is just part of our lives. Women fought hard for equality. In the 1920s, women marched for the right to vote, and they continued to fight for equal rights in the 1960s and '70s. Women wanted to be seen and treated equally in the work force and at home. During this struggle for equality, we understandably gave up a lot of what was considered feminine. We wanted to be taken seriously and respected for our abilities and contributions, so we adopted more masculine characteristics. During this time, some women may have been taught by a strong feminine role model how to depend less on men and to become self-sufficient. I am all for women being equal and doing whatever they want with their lives. We have paid a price, though, for spending so much time in masculine energy. We seem to have an "either/or" mentality sometimes. We try to be feminine when we are going out on a date or on a special occasion but suppress our feminine side on a daily basis. We get into a habit of acting in masculine energy, and we forget how to be feminine. We can become confused in our roles and lose an important part of ourselves. We forget that to be feminine is our true nature, and it is ok to act feminine and be feminine and still be successful in the outside world. We may have to take on more masculine traits in our daily lives, but we can keep that feminine energy at our core and feel feminine all day long on the inside. When we get back together with our partners, it is important to feel and act feminine.

We can get out of touch with our feminine energy. It is important for us to find a way to get back in touch with this side of ourselves. I have found lately that in my relationships, I am too quick to do and to handle things myself and not allow others to help me. I am thinking of giving to them and not allowing them enough space to give to me. This comes from spending so much time being the only one and needing to handle things. I was a single mom for two years and got into the habit of taking care of things myself. Now it is time for me to give over some of that to the guy in my life. I love accomplishing things, but it is exhausting without balance. I love being around masculine energy because then I tap into my feminine energy and feel "at home." I relax and am able just to be and receive. It rejuvenates me! It also creates great passion in my relationship. No one has to tell you how to be feminine. You already are inside. It is a matter of tapping into this energy and finding what works for you. There is no specific definition of what feminine energy looks like. Each woman will have her own version. The key is to find what works for you. What do you need to do to feel more feminine?

When we are in that energy, we help men to feel and to get in touch with their hearts and emotions. It helps them express themselves. They may not share this with us outwardly, but they will be able to feel more. It is important for us to be vulnerable and open with our guys, so they can feel comfortable enough to share their emotions and feelings. Men cannot connect with us when we are in our heads instead of our hearts. Remember that men are looking for a safe place to land at the end of the day. Our soft sides are part of what attracted them to us in the beginning. Now we need to continue to act in that role. Women have to work harder in some ways because we have to change gears from acting in masculine energy all day to regaining our feminine energy with our partners at the end of the day.

When I am working with someone who is having trouble doing this, I suggest she create a ritual to help her. If you work outside of the home, do something on the way home to help you change gears. If you are already at home, you will do the same thing before your guy gets home. Maybe play some music that makes you feel feminine, or even just thinking about your guy can help. At the end of the day, a bath or shower can be very beneficial. Maybe light some candles and have music you like in your bedroom. Put something on that makes you feel feminine. Do this for yourself and for your partner.

It is important for us to give up some control and stop managing, controlling, and over-giving in our relationships. This causes men to feel disrespected, and it hurts the relationship. It takes courage to be feminine and give up this control. It is important to remember femininity is vulnerable but not weak, and it takes courage to be vulnerable. I am in no way suggesting that you have no say-so in your relationship. I am suggesting that during your time with your guy, you find ways to tap into that feminine energy that is your natural way of being. I am suggesting that there is a balance we need to find between doing and being. Women love creating and accomplishing things, but being in masculine energy all the time is tiring. Being in the presence of masculine energy allows us to relax and to receive. This revitalizes and rejuvenates us. Surrendering to masculine energy encourages our guys to be more masculine and to do for us. This is their true nature. We can do this while still being confident and strong on the inside. As a matter of fact, that confidence and strength is very attractive to our guys. We talked earlier about the fact that men want to please us and do for us. We need to allow them to do so. Using feminine energy will make them feel closer to us and make us more attractive to them. It will also increase the desire and passion in our relationships. We will talk more in a later chapter about how this energy creates sparks and passion and why this is so important. For now, keep in mind that this is how we keep the passion alive and find balance for ourselves. It is sexy to be around masculine energy.

Make a list of things that make you feel feminine. What can you do to help the transition from "doing" to "being" when you are spending time with your guy? Some examples to get you started include lighting candles while having dinner. Take a warm bath and use scented bath salts or freshen your body with scented lotion. Play soft music before bed. Enjoy a glass of wine with your guy or simply sit outside and enjoy the sunset together. For something a bit more in depth, have your guy plan a date night, and let him take care of all the details. Allowing your guy to take the lead will make him feel needed and trusted and will allow you to relax and enjoy your time together. Remember that it is all about shifting gears from masculine to feminine energy. Be creative and have fun. Try it and see what happens in your relationship.

For me, relaxing with my guy is my favorite part of the day. I love accomplishing things all day, but I really love putting that aside and tapping into that feminine energy. It really does rejuvenate me. I look forward every night to taking a hot shower and putting on lotion that smells good. I might light a candle or put on something feminine. Getting into bed and putting aside everything else and changing roles is so rewarding. It is rewarding for me and great for my relationship. The message to my guy is clear: this is his time, and I am really happy to be there with him. How we spend that time is not as important as the feeling of being together. All the worries of the day disappear, and I do not feel the need to accomplish anything except to be there for my relationship. It is probably the one thing I missed the most when I was single.

Exercise

- ♥ What makes you feel feminine? Make a list.
- ♥ How can you tap into that feminine side? What can you do to transition from "doing" to "being" when you are with your partner?
- ♥ What routine can you adopt at the end of the day to help you get out of your head and into your heart and body? Start practicing it daily.

❝ *Understanding, truth, words of support, laughter, as well as time alone and silence are keys to a successful relationship. Talk when it's time; be quiet when it's time. Always stay interested and remember the word and feeling of "love" should never be taken lightly.* **❞**

Glenn P.

❝ *My relationship works because we are truly great friends who promise to treat each other with mutual trust and respect at all times. Also we always speak up right away when one or both are unhappy about anything in the relationship.* **❞**

– Larry G.

❝ *Be respectful of each other and each other's thoughts and opinions. Even when you disagree, give them the respect they deserve. Talk about issues that come up until you come to a solution that you both can live with. Respect goes a long way.* **❞**

– Kathleen B.

❝ *In over twelve years of blissful marriage, which I never thought I would be so lucky to have, I believe our success is unwavering TRUST! My husband and I may have disagreements, we may make mistakes and even argue* *(although rarely!), but the glue for us has been constantly communicating about EVERYTHING. The safe haven of never being afraid to share whatever is on our minds, even controversial opinions or sensitive personal feelings, creates such a solid foundation of trust. I do not allow myself to ever doubt how much he desires ME as a mate. I strive every day to show him how awesome he is and how I support him in everything, so that he knows how much I appreciate the man he is for me and for our children. It's my belief that the more I build him up (daily!), the more he'll return that devotion.* **"**

- Kerry H.

The more you understand,
appreciate, and love him, the more he
will appreciate and love you.

Communication can be one
of the most effective ways
to create and keep a strong,
healthy relationship.

Unstoppable Communication

End Power Struggles

Open communication is essential for a healthy relationship. Communication can be one of the most effective ways to create and keep a strong, healthy union. Talking is important in keeping us aware of our partners' needs, discussing life changes, working out problems, and negotiating and settling disagreements. If done the right way, communication is healthy and beneficial to the relationship; however, there are times when it can become harmful. Negative communication not only makes a relationship difficult, but also can be the catalyst to the end of a partnership. This is one of the top reasons marriages deteriorate and couples seek counseling. We need to feel heard and understood; otherwise, we do not feel loved.

Communication can be a challenge in relationships. Couples talk but do not always communicate effectively with each other. Our positive interactions must outweigh the negative ones; otherwise, one or both partners will begin to avoid conversations and ultimately avoid the relationship. Be sure to speak positively to and about your partner. Give compliments and be genuine about them. It is also very important to express appreciation. This does not always have to be an elaborate production. Just saying thanks for the little, day-to-day activities can mean a lot to your partner. It is also important to take time to talk about your day. Use the time after the kids are in bed or over dinner to tell each other about work or other important areas in your lives. It is a nice way to wrap up a busy day. Show each other support and encouragement. Remember that you are in this together! Adding positive communication to your day on a regular basis is very important for your relationship. Incorporating all the things we have talked about so far in the book really will set the tone for your relationship. There are going to be times when you need to resolve conflicts or discuss issues, and it is important to learn how to do this successfully. Unresolved issues eventually deteriorate relationships, which is what we want to avoid.

Resolving Conflicts: Fighting Fair

Fortunately, anyone can learn to communicate better. A great place to start is learning how to have a productive and positive discussion, even when you disagree or are not happy with the other person. Here are some basic ground rules and some suggestions on how to have better conversations.

The first thing you can do to improve communication is to connect emotionally with your partner. The closer you feel to each other, the better the communication will be. The happier you are in your relationship in general, the better the communication and the more you and your partner will feel heard. This is where the secrets in the previous chapters come into play. When you are appreciating your partner and letting him know all he does right, it will be easier to have discussions when things need to be addressed. If most of your communication is positive, your partner will be more receptive to making compromises or negotiating when necessary. If you are working every day to make your relationship a priority and let your partner know how much he means to you, you will already have this emotional connection. If you do not, that might need to be the first step before you start addressing issues. I understand that you want to tell him what he is doing wrong, so he can fix it. I have found over and over again with clients that they need to connect in a positive way first before negotiations can take place. Women need to feel loved, and men need to feel respected. They must feel that they and the relationship are a priority, or communication will not go well. I learned this a long time ago and have found it to be very successful for me and for my clients. Take the time to try this in your relationship. It doesn't have to be complex. Try telling your partner at the end of each day how much you appreciate what he does, or say thank you for even the smallest things such as help with a chore. Making your partner feel appreciated is a big step in feeling connected. Once you have that connection, then you can move forward to addressing issues as they arise.

When the time comes, it is important to pick the right time and place to have the conversation. Don't ask your guy to discuss something as soon as he walks in the door from work or when he is watching his favorite TV show. You will not get the reaction you are looking for. Make sure it is a good time for both of you to talk and that you have some uninterrupted time together. You may need to let your partner know you want to discuss something and then pick a time in the near future to do so. Start by asking if it is good time to talk. Allowing your partner to have a say in when you talk can make a lot of difference in the outcome. If it is not a good time, don't push it. Designate a time to talk in the near future. We will go into this further when we discuss how men and women differ in regard to communication in the next chapter, but for now, keep in mind that timing is important.

Now that you are ready to have your conversation, the first and most important rule is to allow your anger to subside before the discussion. Before giving your emotions a voice, let them calm down a few notches. You are not thinking clearly when you are upset. Do something to calm down and give yourself time before acting.

When we communicate out of anger, we are more likely to say the wrong thing or say something we regret. Our partners go into defensive mode when talked to out of anger, and their brains do not think logically. Many arguments end harshly and may lead to even more frustration and an unproductive conversation. We seldom resolve things and may become more upset, and the original issue can be lost. It can take on a life of its own. When you feel angry or upset with your partner, take some time to calm down and consider why you are frustrated or angry. I find frequently that the catalyst for my anger is not really what the true issue is all about. I need some space and time to think about what is truly bothering me. I might think I am upset because my partner did or did not do something, but really I am feeling neglected or unloved, and that is the underlying issue that I need to address. Now once I understand that, I may or may not need to address it with him. Sometimes what is below the surface can involve issues of trust, love, respect, loyalty, etc. Also, once you calm down, you might decide the issue really is not that big of a deal. You might be having a bad day, or you might be hungry or tired. Whatever the reason, sometimes once you are calmer, you may decide the conversation isn't necessary; however, don't let things build up and get out of control. If it is a discussion you need to have because you aren't happy, then make time for it. Remember to choose your battles. You want most of your time together to be positive.

Choosing your words carefully is essential. Words can be very strong and hurtful if said in the wrong way and at the wrong time. How you communicate your feelings and thoughts can make a huge difference in the outcome. Never use harsh words, name-calling, or belittling each other. Talk to the other person as you would like to be talked to. Remember that what is said cannot be unsaid, and people forgive but do not easily forget. Realize that the other person is not you. Something else to keep in mind is that he may not even understand why you are upset. He does not have the same life experiences you do. He may not have the same expectations either. How you approach your partner with issues becomes very important. Before you get angry that your partner does not understand you or see the issue the same way you do, stop for a minute and try to find out if you are on the same page. You may need to explain a little more about why you are upset. It is also important to take responsibility for your role in the issue being discussed. Don't blame, criticize, or tell your partner what he did wrong even if this is an issue he is responsible for. This can be difficult, especially if you are upset. What is most important here is to take responsibility for your own feelings. In turn, you will open the space for your partner to feel safe and to hear you.

The best way to do this is to use "I" statements instead of "you" when addressing an issue. This stops the attacking or blaming of the other person. Plan ahead of time how you can best phrase comments, so you can get your point across without putting your partner on the defensive. One example of this is a partner who is always late, while you like to be on time. You are feeling upset because he is late again! Instead of speaking out of anger and telling him how upset you are because he is always late, try a different approach. Let him know how important it is for you to be on time and how you feel when you are late. This keeps it in the "I" statement form. Remember: he might not mind being late. Then once you have expressed your feelings and have taken responsibility for them, you are in a better position to ask for a suggested solution of how you can be on time when you go places together.

Keep the current issue the only issue and leave the past in the past. Bringing up past issues or examples is counterproductive and will shut down the conversation quickly. The other person will become defensive and stop listening to what you have to say and will begin to focus on his defense. Even if this is a pattern, bringing that into the conversation may make you feel better at the moment but will not help solve the issue.

Your partner needs to feel heard in order for communication to go well. Stop multi-tasking! This means no checking your phone or watching TV during the conversation. Make eye contact and let your partner know you are listening. When your partner is talking to you, respond to him, so he knows that you are paying attention. To really listen means you need to just listen! This is hard to do because we naturally start thinking of a response or a solution once our partners start to talk. It is important to give him your full attention, which means not judging what he is saying as right or wrong. Even if you do not find this pleasant, it will go faster with a more positive outcome if you can let your partner know he has your attention.

Now that you have voiced your feelings appropriately and listened to your partner, it is time to ask for a solution or to give advice if appropriate. It may be better to ask your partner for a suggested solution, especially if you are talking to a guy. Remember that they are problem solvers by nature. Try to come up with a solution or a compromise if at all possible. Sometimes, though, you have to be okay with agreeing to disagree. Not all issues can be compromised on or solved. Sometimes partners are two unique individuals with different needs and viewpoints and will disagree. If it is a practical issue like picking up the children from school or getting the housework done, then you may need time to work out a solution. Allow your partner time to think about it and pick a time to talk later.

End the conversation with something positive such as a hug or a kiss. This will help bring closure to the discussion and serve as a sign that you and your partner can move forward. It will help you both feel better about the whole experience and make you both more willing to address issues in the future.

Learn to ask and not make demands of the other person. Choose your battles, communicate with respect, take responsibility for your feelings, and apologize when necessary. Also, remember to share all emotions with your partner, not just the anger or your frustrations. Share the joy, bliss, and love, and what you like, love, and respect about him. We all have disagreements. It is part of every relationship; however, there are ways to turn arguments into positive discussions. Approaching disagreements calmly and with open ears may teach us something about our partners and even ourselves! You can both come away from these communications feeling a closer connection and more love.

Your exercise for this chapter is to practice fighting fair!

More Differences Between Men and Women

When it comes to communication, men and women are different. Not understanding those differences can lead to confusion, hurt feelings, and a great deal of frustration. This can be a major barrier to problem solving. Let's spend some time discussing some of the differences that might help you not only understand your partner better but also be able to communicate more effectively. The differences in our brains and the way we think also apply to communication. Women tend to use verbal communication more and to incorporate a number of topics in a conversation. We do not separate emotions and facts as much as men. Remember that our thought process is complex, and if you were to draw what it looks like on paper, it might look like a plate of spaghetti. Everything is connected, including thoughts and emotions. Men compartmentalize and usually focus on one thought at a time, so they find our type of communication frustrating.

I have noticed that in my conversations with men, when I change topics quickly, incorporate too many topics in one conversation, or ramble on with lots of ideas, they get this far-away look in their eye or give me some kind of clue that I have lost their interest. I handle sessions with men and women in a different way, taking into account how they process information. That said, as I talk about these differences, I am speaking in general terms and realize that not everyone fits these criteria exactly. My goal here is to give you some information that will help you understand communication styles that affect most men and women.

Women for the most part will seek out others to talk to when they have a problem or are feeling stressed about a situation. This is one way they can release the stress and feel better. Women talk things through in order to solve problems. They are using both sides of their brains during this process. Frequently, they need to release emotions first and then talk about all the possible ideas and solutions in order to come to an end and move forward.

Women do this in their personal lives, but you can also see this in the workplace. Women are typically team players and like to ask more questions and seek others' ideas before moving forward. This is one way women build rapport and feel close to others. They have a strong desire to feel heard and understood. It is important for women to have other women in their lives with whom to communicate and share issues and emotions. Being able to talk through things first with other women may be beneficial before approaching their partners, allowing them to work through situations and condense discussions with the men in their lives. The important thing to remember here is to use other women to talk with about the issue in order to gain clarity not to talk poorly about your partners.

Sometimes when women are talking, all they really need is to be heard and to feel supported. They may not be looking for a solution at all. This is hard for men to understand since they are solution oriented. This causes discord in relationships when a woman only wants to vent and feel heard, but her partner tries to solve a problem. He may feel disrespected because she does not seem interested in his solutions. I tell couples that if she is discussing a problem that involves emotions, just let her vent and support her. If something is broken, then offer to fix it. I know this is a simplistic scenario, but many times, women walk away from a conversation even more frustrated because they simply needed to be heard. For men who are unsure of how to proceed, just ask her.

Men generally communicate in a different way. Men do not like drama in their communication for the most part. They prefer to avoid the emotions and get to the bottom line as quickly as possible. When you are asking your partner for a good time to discuss a problem, it is helpful if you can let him know that you are not upset and reassure him that there will not be drama in the conversation. It is very important not to criticize, judge, offer advice, warn, coax, or try to change him during these conversations. It will not move the conversation forward in a positive direction. Conversations with men need to be shorter and more to the point. I suggest giving him the *Reader's Digest* version of the problem. If you can keep the conversation short and drama free, he will be much more likely to hear you and to respond in a positive way.

Men want to be successful in all areas of their lives, and this also applies to communication. If he feels he won't be successful at finding a solution, he may shut down or stop communicating. This is why it is so important that women understand their guys better. You need to learn how to talk to him regarding disagreements, so he does not feel attacked or that his opinion doesn't matter. Women want to feel heard, and this is the way to accomplish that while also allowing him to feel good about the communication. It is a win/win situation. Because men want to be successful, they will sometimes take longer to come up with a solution. Women talk until they find a solution, but men often need quiet time to do the same. They prefer to think of all the possibilities alone and then discuss a solution once they have their thoughts together. I have noticed often that women interpret this as the guy not caring or not being interested. They do not understand that he just problem-solves in a different way. You might need to agree to meet later to discuss the issue further. Then give your guy some time alone, so he can think and process. It actually means he cares enough to want to take the time to do so.

In order to have more productive communication with men, it is beneficial for women to be in their feminine energy. When we are in that energy, we are truly listening, and they will feel heard. We are not "doing" but are appropriately expressing our emotions and thoughts. This can be a hard transition for us because we spend so much of our time doing and problem solving all day. This is a switch that may not come easily. Some women feel they are giving in or giving something up when they make this switch. The opposite is really true. You are getting in touch with your inner feminine side and utilizing the differences between men and women for a mutually successful outcome. You are partners and want to be a team.

When you are in that feminine energy and are communicating with your guy, you will give up trying to control him and the outcome of the situation. In order to truly listen, this is essential. You will appreciate him and his uniqueness instead of criticizing. You will remember to show respect, so he will want to stay engaged in the conversation and not withdraw. You will also learn to take no for an answer and agree to disagree sometimes. This is often the hardest part to do and to feel okay doing it. It really takes looking at the big picture in regard to the relationship and keeping things in perspective. Remember that the relationship and your commitment to each other is the ultimate goal, and most of your issues really are just small things. Some compromises will go your way, and some will not. As good as it might feel to always get your own way, it is not good for the relationship as a whole. No one wants to be in a relationship where they always have to give in or feel they are wrong. Accepting compromise or disagreement is easier to do when you allow your emotions to calm down before you have the discussion. You can see things more clearly when you are not in the midst of anger or frustration.

Advice from Real Unstoppable Relationships

66 *Unstoppable relationships require unhindered communication and undeterred humility. There is no room for competition or stubbornness.* **99**

- Dena. B.

66 *Good relationships are founded on the idea that listening is more important than being right.* **99**

- Paul C.

66 *We can talk about anything. I feel safe and understood. He cares enough to really listen to me. I feel accepted and loved for who I am, and I love him for who he is. I feel cherished by him.* **99**

- Donna M.

66 *Keep the lines of communication open always and have a good sense of humor. We have been together over twenty years and still get excited to see each other! Also, we can't wait to share our triumphs and lessons.* **99**

– Lianne H.

66 *When my husband and I got married, I noticed that he told me thank you even for the small things I did around the house. He would express his gratitude for the dinner I cooked or for folding his laundry or even reminding him about our weekend plans. At first, it was a little strange, but I quickly caught on and started saying thank you, as well, for all of the things he did for me. I figured it was a newlywed thing and would eventually wear off. After all, I grew up in a wonderful home with two very loving and giving parents, but they never said thank you to each other. I suppose I thought thank you was implied. Fast forward ten years later, and my husband still tells me thank you every day for something I have done for the family. He tells me all of the time that being a stay-at-home mom is a lot of work, and he appreciates what I do for the family because it allows him to do what he needs to do for his job. I came to realize that so many relationships lack gratitude. We rely so much on our partners for support that we forget that thank you can mean so much. Why is it that we will willingly show appreciation to total strangers for holding the door for us, but we don't say thank you to our partners when they* *fix the squeaky door handle, plan dinner, or help us with household chores? I believe that showing appreciation to our partners is simple but very important when it comes to keeping the relationship happy and healthy!* **"**

- Nancy L.

Couples who make passion
a priority are more patient,
appreciative, and forgiving
with each other.

Unstoppable Love and Passion

Now that we have talked about making your relationship a priority, understanding and appreciating the differences between men and women, and how to communicate effectively, we can move on to the last secret in an unstoppable relationship. Intimacy and passion are not just for the beginning of relationships. It is even more important as the relationship progresses to make time for passion and romance. You cannot have an unstoppable relationship without them. After all, intimacy is what defines a relationship as "intimate" rather than just a friendship!

In the beginning of a relationship in the romantic phase, your bodies are full of those "feel good" hormones making passion and intimacy easier. Once you have been together for a period of time and those hormones naturally start to decrease, you need to proactively create passion in your relationship. In the beginning, it is the differences between you that create sparks. Over time, however, love develops. You become more comfortable with each other, and passion may begin to subside. Many people do not believe that relationships can maintain love and passion. They believe that it naturally fades, and there is nothing they can do about it; however, the truth is that relationships die without love and passion. You become frustrated and resentful with each other and start focusing on the things you do not like about your partner. Life gets in the way or gets complicated, and you have so many demands on your time and energy that intimacy takes a back seat. You can feel like it is one more thing to do, one more chore. You come home tired at the end of the day and still have so much to do. You just want to be alone and rest. It seems easier to find reasons not to be intimate.

There are numerous reasons why it is good to keep passion alive in your relationship or renew it if it has gone away. The hormone oxytocin that is released during sex creates a bonding feeling between couples. Besides feeling good, this hormone also helps you focus on how much you love your partner. Couples who have active sex lives focus more on the positive attributes of their partners. They talk more, communicate better, have more fun, and are happier in general with their relationships. Intimacy is not just for him, ladies. You will find that you benefit from that connection as well. Sex makes you happier. Having sex with your partner makes you desire more sex and intimacy. Can you see how having more intimacy can help you in all areas of your relationship? You will feel more connected to your partner. You will have more patience and be more tolerant of his differences. You will feel more bonded and closer emotionally, and it will be easier to let the little things go while keeping a positive perspective. Added to that are the physical benefits of making love. It is aerobic and good exercise. It is also relaxing and helps to reduce stress. It is a nice distraction from the rest of the world and the stress of everyday life. It can be beneficial to your health and happiness! The key is to create passion with intention!

It All Begins With You: How to Feel Comfortable in Your Own Skin

You need to create passion in your relationship, and it all starts with you. It is important first to be attractive for yourself. This is not just about your appearance. It is how you feel about yourself, your self-esteem and confidence. Beauty has so much to do with confidence and feeling sensual no matter your age or body type. It is also about your emotions, attitude, and state of mind. Passion and zest for life are sexy! What truly gives you pleasure in life? What makes you feel sensual and feminine? Do you have daily rituals that help you to connect with your body and feel sexy? Most women I talk to do not. We can get so busy working and taking care of our families that we lose touch with our own femininity. If you work outside of the home, you may need to act more like one of the guys at work. In order to be seen as an equal, you don't want to be soft and feminine or sexy in the workplace. Even if you stay at home, you are busy taking care of children, which is very feminine, but not in a way that makes you feel sensual or sexy!

Women spend a great deal of their time in masculine energy. When we are in masculine energy, we are in our heads focusing on ideas, chores, and problems to solve. This is not a frame of mind that is conducive to feeling sensual and feminine. It does not make us overly attractive to our partners either. They may appreciate all we are doing, but the spark of passion comes from our feminine energy meeting their masculine energy. It is hard for us to be in the mood for romance when we are thinking and doing. We need to connect to our bodies and tap into that core feminine energy. This will help us to feel more sensual, and it will get the sparks flying and the hormones racing. It is very important to quiet our minds in order to make the transition from doing all day to being when we are spending quality time with our partners. This is why having a ritual each day is so important. It is a signal that there is more to you than accomplishing things; there is also the soft, vulnerable, feminine side.

I encourage you to spend time every day looking in the mirror and feeling confident and beautiful. Learn to appreciate all the curves to your body. Learn to accept your body as it is. This might take some time, but keep it up until you feel sexy. Learn to replace negative self-talk with self-love. Do things daily to care for your body and to make you feel good about yourself. Men do not care about all the little things we see as flaws in our bodies. They probably do not even notice them. They love us the way we are and want us to feel the same about our bodies and to share that with them. Dress each day in a way that will help you to feel stunning in your own unique style. I encourage women to always wear pretty undergarments, even if you are the only one to see them. It starts your day feeling feminine and sensual. Purchase pretty bras and panties that you can wear every day. Do this for yourself, and if you decide to share it with your guy, that is an added bonus.

It is easier to tap into sensuality when we have a strong sense of ourselves and feel confident and beautiful. I want you to learn to take care of yourself. Take care of the details that make you feel beautiful. There is a sexy, feminine person inside each woman; she just needs permission to come out. This will look different for every woman. Find the sexy you that feels right instead of trying to hold yourself to some outside standard. Create daily rituals that take care of you inside and out. When a relationship is new, we take great care in how we present ourselves and how much attention we give to our partners. Then once we are married, we put in less time and attention. It really should be the opposite. Once you are married or have been together for a while, you want to put in even more effort into keeping your partner and the relationship.

Pay attention to your attitude as well as your looks. Beauty also comes from the inside. No matter what you do to the outside, you will not feel confident and feminine unless you feel that way on the inside. So what steps do you need to take to feel confident in yourself? Do you need to have more passion for life in general? Do you need to add something new to your life, a new hobby or interest? Do you need to take steps to exercise and eat better? Do you need to freshen up your look and start taking better care of your appearance? Remember that passion and a zest for life are very sexy! Start making small changes to add more excitement to your life and to your relationship. We have been taught that when we work hard, we are rewarded. That is true, and we should work to achieve those goals and have the things we want. But what about pleasure? How many people plan and make time consciously to have fun? When we do, does that fun involve our partners? Does it involve intimacy and passion? Our relationships should be safe havens, places to end our days with love and passion!

Exercise

- What changes can you make to your life that will help you to feel feminine and sexy?
- What are some things you can do to feel more confident and comfortable with your body? Look in the mirror daily and say affirming statements.
- What daily ritual will you add that helps you to get out of your head and to reconnect with your body at the end of the day?
- What hobbies or new interests can you pursue?
- What do you need to do to feel better about yourself physically? Maybe more exercise, a change of diet, or a new look?
- How will you add more fun to your life?

Reignite Passion

When I am talking to men and women about passion in their relationships, I find two very common beliefs. One is that they do not believe that passion lasts in relationships. They have been told and believe that intimacy and passion with their partners declines naturally as we age and our relationships progress. I have heard from some men that they believe women are no longer interested in sex after they have children. Men definitely want more passion and intimacy from their partners, but they have just given up the hope of having that in their relationships again.

I think that many women also believe that it is just part of life and that they will be less interested in sex as they get older. The other belief that I frequently encounter is that most couples are happy with their love lives and feel other parts of the relationship are lacking. They believe most people have satisfying love lives, so they feel embarrassed to admit theirs needs help. Women may believe that they cannot keep their guys satisfied because men will always want more than women are willing to give, so these women quit trying. Men may have been turned down so many times that they quit trying. One or both partners may not be satisfied with the sexual activities they are engaging in. Not having a satisfactory love life, no matter what the reason, is not something most people feel comfortable sharing with others or even their partners. I find that most couples do not talk about this topic with each other or do anything to try to improve the situation. Maybe they did in the beginning, but then they became frustrated and quit trying, or they just do not know where to start in order to rejuvenate their love lives. Relationships die without love and passion. They become more like a friendship, at best. This is not why we entered into our marriages, and they are not relationships that most couples are happy with.

We are not taught how to have long-term relationships that are full of passion. We learn a great deal from books, movies, and TV shows about what passionate relationships look like in the beginning. How often do you read or see stories about couples who have loving, passionate relationships ten years or more after they are married? Do you and your friends talk about your love lives once the honeymoon phase wears off? The answer to that is probably yes but only if you are complaining about your love lives. It is not part of our everyday lives to discuss passion in our relationships as they progress. Unfortunately, passion and intimacy do tend to naturally decline in most relationships unless we do something consciously to change that. We have talked about why it is so important to have passion in our relationships; now let's talk about how to rejuvenate it.

One of the first things we must do is tap into our feminine and masculine energy when we are alone with our partners. For men, this means taking the initiative, but sometimes men quit doing this because they have been turned down so many times. For women, this means being open to receiving, being soft and feminine. We need to encourage our guys to show us how much they love us and want to be with us! It is sexy to be wanted by our guys. Remember from the previous chapter that it is very important for women to develop a routine to help them tap back into this feminine energy. We need this balance in our lives, and our relationships need it as well. The differences between men and women and the differences between the masculine and feminine energy attract us to each other and help us to feel more passionate toward each other. For women, it is hard to feel passionate when we are busy planning, thinking, and doing. I know we have brains that are hard to shut off at the end of the day. It is easier for men to shift gears and be in the moment, especially when it comes to sex. It is just as important for us to do the same thing, though. We need to find ways to help us do that. We need to get out of our heads and into our hearts. I want you to make a plan for what you can do each day to help you feel more feminine. What small things can you implement today? Find ways to feel feminine and sensual.

Just like in other areas, men and women think and act differently when it comes to intimacy. For women, intimacy starts in the heart; we need to feel wanted and loved. Attention is an aphrodisiac for women. It really starts early in the day for us, not at night right before we have sex. It is about how we feel in general about our guys and our relationships. Women want to be romanced throughout the day, every day. We want to be thought about and noticed and appreciated. Women need to feel connected to their partners and their relationships in order to feel passionate.

What do you do if you do not feel this way in your relationship? There are a couple of ways to address this. First, remember everything you learned in the previous chapters! It is important to stop telling your guy what he is doing wrong or what you think he needs to do better. A more subtle approach is in order. You could give him this book to read, of course, if that is something he would be interested in. But if not, you can accomplish a great deal by changing *your* thoughts and actions. *Your* thoughts and actions are the two things you have control over, and it is your thoughts that ultimately create your reality.

Let's start with those daily activities that help you to feel more feminine. Women need more time to warm up to the idea of intimacy; we need to start early in the day thinking about and looking forward to the evening. Just by preparing yourself mentally, you will approach your guy with more feminine energy, and he will notice the difference. We will talk about more specific ideas for how to do this later. The important part for now is you will feel different, and that is the first step.

You can also let him know what he is doing that makes you feel special. Catch him doing things right and let him know how much you appreciate it. If he feels like he is doing something right, he is more likely to do it again. You can also talk about wanting to have more passion in your relationship. Give him ideas of what might help you feel more in the mood. He might really have no idea that by helping with the dishes or getting the kids to bed, he is enabling you to take a hot bath and transition from thinking and doing to being, enabling you to feel ready for intimacy. Just remember that if you give him a suggestion and he tries it, make sure you follow through. Let him know how much you appreciate it, AND make sure it does lead to some form of intimacy.

Now, I want you to understand more about him and how important intimacy is to him. How often do you tell your guy no, assuming he is still being assertive in asking? I have noticed in relationships that women will say yes to requests at work, from their children, from church, from friends, from neighbors, from the school PTA, but when their partners ask for their time and attention, they will quickly and easily say no! I do not believe that women understand what this does to guys. We do not understand how much this hurts them and makes them feel unloved. It is similar to them ignoring us and not giving us any attention. Physical connection with us—in the form of sex—is one of the top relationship priorities for men. It is right there next to the respect we talked about earlier. It is one of the most important ways men feel loved and appreciated by us. It makes them feel like Superman to know that we think they are attractive and that we are attracted to them.

Your partner wants to please you and to share intimacy with you. It is the one thing that only you can give him, the one thing that only the two of you share together! It is much more important to men than most women realize. A satisfying sexual relationship with you does more than just bond him to you and make him feel good about the relationship; it also affects how he feels at work and about life in general. When he feels desired and wanted in his relationship, he is more confident in all areas of his life. Men who are flirted with and who feel wanted by their partners are much happier in their relationships and in life in general. So knowing how much this means to your partner, why would you want to say no to him? It may seem overwhelming especially if your relationship currently lacks this kind of intimacy, and I am not suggesting that this should become an obligation that you don't benefit from as well; however, there are many ways to improve this area of your relationship for you and your partner. We will discuss ideas for how to make you want this as much as he does. It may begin as something you do for your partner, but it will not stay that way!

Please try and keep in mind that this is just as much for you as it is for your partner. Just by getting in touch with your feminine energy, you will find more balance in your life. I find that no matter how tired I am from the overload of thinking and doing every day, getting in touch with my feminine energy refreshes me so I can spend quality and intimate time with my guy. I benefit from this time with him as much as he does. I feel more connected and more loved. I feel important to him and that our relationship is a priority. I feel more in love and closer to him emotionally and physically. I find I am more relaxed, energized, and rejuvenated. My guy is not the only one with a smile on his face; I feel happier with life in general, and that happiness extends into the next day as well. Women also feel more secure in their relationships when there is more intimacy. Those bonding hormones that are released during sex make both partners feel more connected and happier with each other. This is essential for your relationship. Couples who make passion a priority have more appreciation for each other, more patience. They focus on the positives, and are more forgiving with each other, which are all essential elements for an unstoppable relationship.

I want you to consider adding some form of intimacy to your life on a daily basis. Try not to let this overwhelm you; this does not mean you have to spend hours having amazing sex every night. That probably is not realistic. I do want you to say "yes" to your guy, though, most evenings. I do understand that you might be sick some days or have some other extenuating circumstances, but that will not be the norm. I want you to be open to connecting physically with your partner daily. This can start with small things. It can be an added hug and kiss, not just a quick one, though. Try a ten-second kiss; this will actually get your hormones flowing, helping you to feel more in the mood. Maybe add some snuggling time at the end of the day while you watch TV or talk about what happened in your day. By starting with small gestures, you and your partner will reap the rewards, and that will encourage you to want to add more to your relationship. Just get started and watch the momentum build!

Exercise

Go back to your list of ways to feel more feminine and implement something new!

- ❤ What can you do daily to feel more sensual and sexy?
- ❤ What can your partner do to help you get in the mood for romance? Tell him in a nice way and let him know why. He will be excited to help.
- ❤ Be a "yes" to your guy! Add small shows of affection to your day; remember that 10 second kiss? Spend quality time together on a daily basis.

Sexy Nights

Now that we have talked about why passion and intimacy are so important to your relationship, my hope is that you are ready to start incorporating more into your life. I want you to start small at first. Once you make this a habit and a regular part of your relationship, I am convinced it will be well worth your time and effort, and you will never want to go back to where you started!

You cannot wait for the right time to add more intimacy to your busy life. You have to create passion with intention, or it gets pushed to the side. Small changes will make a difference and will help motivate you to continue. You can start by making it a priority to add some playfulness to your relationship on a daily basis. We have already talked about adding those hugs and kisses to your day and to increase the length of them. No more quick pecks on the cheek or a quick hug. It needs to be meaningful and, yes, sexy! So big bear hugs and lingering kisses are in order at least twice a day; aim for in the morning before separating and when you are reunited at the end of the day. This does more than add a physical connection; it shows your partner how important he is to you. You are taking time out to give him your undivided attention. Maybe add something whispered in his ear periodically. It can be something as simple as to tell your partner that he looks nice, or you could hint at wanting more physical touch from him soon. Be playful and express yourself in whatever way you are comfortable with, as long as you are adding the physical touch and the playfulness to your routine. I also like for couples to add more physical touch to their routine during times that are not intended to lead to sex. Hold hands, cuddle, put your arm around each other, or add a lingering touch as you pass your partner in the house; any touch that you would both enjoy is great. This will let both partners know that they are wanted, thought of, and that you still find each other attractive and sexy.

Men and women both need to be flirted with on a regular basis. It doesn't take much time to whisper a sweet nothing in your partner's ear or to send him a flirty text or email during the day. I love the idea of using texting to add some playfulness to your relationship. It can be a great way to flirt during the day. I like to send quick, flirty texts when I am in the middle of a meeting or at an event. It really shows my guy that even though I am busy, I am still thinking of him. This is a great way to spice up your relationship and to build anticipation for intimacy later in the day. You can also send loving texts during the day. Just a short text to say, "I love you," or "I miss you," or "I am thinking about you," can go a long way. Flirting can also be a smile and a look you give your partner that says, "I want you; you are mine."

This is just a start, and you can add whatever you like. Flirting can be lots of fun when you are in a relationship because it can be more overt and risqué than when you are dating. Flirting triggers those "feel-good" hormones and makes adding more intimacy to your life seem like a great idea. The more you think about quality time together and adding intimacy to your day, the more you will look forward to it. This helps when you are trying to make it a priority.

We talked earlier about feeling comfortable in your own skin. I talked about dressing in a way that makes you feel feminine. I want to remind you here that this is a great way to help you get in the mood for more intimacy at the end of the day. Start your day wearing something under your clothes that makes you feel sexy. I truly believe that women should always have on underwear that they think is pretty and that makes them feel sexy! You can do this on whatever budget you have. It can be something as simple as a pretty bra with matching panties, or it can be something much sexier if you like. The point is that you should start your day reminding yourself that you are feminine and sexy, and that can take many different forms. Then throughout the day, be aware of what you are wearing under your clothes. Men will tell you that they think of sex throughout the day with no need for reminders, but women tend to need reminders. Men still enjoy them as well, so keep up that flirting and texting!

Now at the end of the day women frequently need a little help switching gears, so they can get out of their heads and switch to feeling feminine and sensual. A routine can help you do that. Some women will put on music that helps them feel sensual while they are driving home from work. They might start fantasizing while they are driving. If you are already at home, I suggest you stop and take a little time to maybe change clothes and freshen up before your partner gets home. Do something for you to help you focus your thoughts on your guy. For years when I was home with young children, before I started dinner in the evening, I would go into the bathroom and freshen up, which would start my anticipation for seeing my husband at the end of the day. It really turned my thoughts from childrearing and working to my relationship. I would start to get excited about seeing him and think about getting that big hug when he walked in the door. It was, I think, an important element of keeping the passion alive in our relationship for twenty-five years.

I also suggest that you have an evening ritual. Taking a bath or hot shower is great for relieving any stress you are still carrying from the day, and the hot water on your skin gets your blood circulating. While you are in the shower or bath, focus your thoughts not on your to-do list but on your partner. It is time to turn your focus inward to your body. Allow yourself to relax and start to think sensual thoughts, maybe even read a sexy novel while soaking in the tub. Let your anticipation start to build for whatever the evening holds. Even if it is just looking forward to some snuggle time before bed. Then put on some lotion that smells good and have some type of self-care routine. You and your body are important. I have a lotion that I use every night, and that smell triggers sensual thoughts for me. You might want to put on something to wear that makes you feel good; this does not have to be what you will sleep in but just something that you feel good in for the evening. The particulars of the routine are not important, but the routine is. This is your time away from work, children, and any other demands, and it is your time to reconnect at the end of the day with your partner.

Add anything else that will help you relax. That may include some yoga, meditation, soft music, candles, a glass of wine, or simply turning down the lights. Create ambiance in your bedroom. Turn off your cell phone and spend time with your partner. Some people will suggest turning off the TV, but I think you can enjoy a show together as long as you are doing it together and are physically connected at the time. That means you need to be snuggled next to each other, holding hands, or perhaps entwining your legs. This is not as much about watching TV as it is sharing some uninterrupted time relaxing and reconnecting.

This time together has to be a priority, so I would like to

suggest that in the beginning at least, you add it to your calendar. You might already have a date night, or maybe you want to add one of those as well. This is not the same as date night, though; this is a date for physical intimacy. Now it could correlate with date night to start. If it is on the calendar, that means you are making it a priority. Making it a priority will ensure it will happen and also help you build anticipation! This is a great start but only a start. I would suggest that you take a look at your love life and plan to start by doubling your time together. If you usually make love on the weekend, add a weeknight to your schedule. Remember that the ultimate goal is to add some form of intimacy to your life daily. This can be something as simple as snuggling during your favorite TV show or just spending some time kissing at the end of the day. It doesn't matter as much what you do as the idea that you are connecting. If your partner is the one who usually initiates the intimacy, then how about you make the suggestion next time. It is important for both partners to show interest in intimacy. That lets the other person know you are not just going along but that you are interested enough to initiate.

Sometimes women tell me that they do not initiate sex as often because they are not in the "mood." This is another difference between men and women. Men are usually able to change gears and be in the mood much easier than women. That is part of the reason women need to start thinking about feeling sensual and sexy earlier in the day and need evening rituals to help them turn off their minds and get back in touch with their bodies. If lack of desire is an issue for you and none of the above suggestions are helping, you might want to talk to your doctor and make sure there is not a medical reason. Illness, hormone imbalance, or even certain medications can affect your desire. You might also read *The Orgasmic Diet* by Marrena Lindberg. This book has some great ideas about how changing your diet and adding some supplements can improve your love life. It not only is a healthy diet (and, yes, you can eat chocolate), but also increases hormones that contribute to feeling sexy and enjoying sex more. So I think it is worth a try.

Finally, I talk to women who say that they like my ideas of more intimacy and understand it would be good for their relationships, but they do not really enjoy having sex with their partners. If this is the case for you, or even if you are bored with your current sexual activities, I suggest you still start with all the above suggestions. Add more fun and flirting to your life. Add more physical touch that does not lead to sex, and spend more time together. Then talk to your partner about adding something new or trying something in a different way. If you are not happy with something, suggest something else. If you are uncomfortable talking about this or do not want to tell your partner you do not like something, initiate what you do like or would like instead. Then after, let him know how much you enjoyed yourself. Your guy wants you to be interested in sex and to enjoy it. He wants to please you. Just like in other areas of your relationship, let him know when he does something you like. If this continues to be an issue for you, it might be time to ask for professional help. Don't let a lack of communication about sex keep your relationship from being unstoppable! I want you to be a "yes" to your guy and to have more intimacy in your relationship, and I want it to be something you enjoy and look forward to.

There are many different ways to add intimacy back into your relationship and to make it a priority. We have discussed a few, but I want you to take it from here and find what works for the two of you. Have fun and be creative. Use fun ways of communication to add intimate moments to your everyday routine. Write love notes or send fun texts. It is important to remember that men and women can be different in every aspect of their relationships, including intimacy. Use those differences to your advantage. The important part of intimacy is to make it a priority and to use it to bring you closer to each other in all areas of your relationship.

Exercise

- Schedule a night for lovemaking! Put it on your schedule as a priority, and start building anticipation. Start by doubling your time together and build from there.
- Add more playfulness and flirting to your relationship.
- Add more physical contact, hand holding, hugging, kissing, or snuggling.
- Add an evening ritual of self-care that will help you relax and get ready to spend time with your partner.
- Talk to your partner about what you like and don't like about your intimate time together. Communicate to improve your love life.
- Have fun together! Sex is one area that you share only with your partner, and it is an important aspect of an unstoppable relationship. So enjoy it.

❝ My husband and I have been together for over fifteen years, and we still get butterflies when we see each other. We flirt with each other like we were dating. We make it a priority to spend time together on a regular basis, without the children. Some of our favorite times together are when we are relaxing, holding hands, hugging, or kissing. Physical intimacy is an important part of our relationship. It helps us feel connected to each other. ❞

- Susan K.

❝ Kiss your wife every day like you love her, not just want her. ❞

- Chris R.

❝ With love and passion in your relationship, you will build confidence in yourself and your partner. With that confidence, you both will fight for that love and passion to remain forever. ❞

- Megan M.

❝ Passion, you see, is not just nice-to-have; it is truly necessary. It is the fire in the engine that keeps your relationship alight. Without passion, you are hibernating, cohabitating. But when there is passion's fire in there—well then, the relationship with THAT type of desire is unstoppable, truly the work of art it is meant to be! ❞

- Sabrina R.

Acknowledgements

I want to thank my dear friend Laura. This book was brought to life sitting around my dining room table having coffee with you. You have been my sounding board, my first editor, and at times my inspiration to keep writing. I would not have had the courage to complete this book without your faith in me.

To SPARK Publications for believing in me and helping make this book a reality, your guidance and expertise was invaluable.

I appreciate all my wonderful friends, coaches, colleagues, and clients who provided me with support and encouragement throughout this process.

To my family, thank you for being patient and encouraging me every step of the way.

About the Author

Lori Ann Davis, MA, CRS
Certified Relationship Specialist, Speaker, Author & Radio Host

Lori has a unique and passionate approach to love and relationships and believes that all people deserve and can have the relationships of their dreams. Her mission is to provide you with the skills you need to have the unstoppable relationship you deserve.

She has over twenty-eight years of experience empowering individuals and couples to live richer, happier lives. She has an in-person, private practice in Charlotte, N.C., and also provides relationship coaching by phone to people throughout the United States. Her practice spans the spectrum from dating and singles to working through divorce to renewing long-term marriages.

In addition to workshops, classes, couples' retreats, and a local singles group, Lori's radio show "Ask Lori" on WGIV/WDRB media has become a popular medium to share relationship information to millions of listeners.

Born and raised in New Orleans, she has a master's degree in clinical psychology from the University of West Florida in Pensacola. For more than twenty years, she was a mental health counselor practicing individual, marriage, and family therapy in Florida.

Now living in Charlotte, Lori is the mother of three daughters and is proud to homeschool her two youngest.

Information about all of Lori's coaching services, other products, blogs, radio show, and events can be found at www.lorianndavis.com.

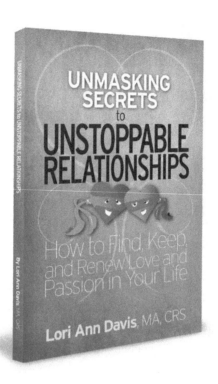

Visit www.lorianndavis.com to:

- ♥ Sign up for Lori's newsletter.
- ♥ Find out about upcoming "Unstoppable Relationship" events, including workshops for singles and couples.
- ♥ Listen to her radio show.
- ♥ Watch her videos.
- ♥ Order the "Unstoppable Relationships" four-CD set.
- ♥ Invite Lori to speak to your women's organization or conference.